Imagining Black Womanhood

Imagining Black Womanhood

The Negotiation
of Power and Identity
within the
Girls Empowerment Project

STEPHANIE D. SEARS

Cover photo courtesy of Harry Cutting Photography

Published by State University of New York Press, Albany

For information, contact State University of New York Press, Albany, NY
www.sunypress.edu

Production by Diane Ganeles
Marketing by Anne M. Valentine

Library of Congress Cataloging-in-Publication Data

Sears, Stephanie D., 1964-
   Imagining Black womanhood : the negotiation of power and identity
within the Girls Empowerment Project / Stephanie D. Sears.
       p. cm.
   Includes bibliographical references and index.
   ISBN 978-1-4384-3327-1 (hardcover : alk. paper)
   ISBN 978-1-4384-3326-4 (pbk. : alk. paper)
   1. Womanism—United States. 2. African American girls. 3. Women,
Black—United States. 4. Identity (Philosophical concept) I. Title.
HQ1197.S43 2010
305.23089'96073—dc22
                                            2009053987

10 9 8 7 6 5 4 3 2 1

Contents

Figures

Preface

"I'm not black, I AM NOT BLACK!"

I'll never forget the day Zoë, my then three-year-old daughter, defiantly shouted these words. As a special treat we had gone to the neighborhood McDonald's to have lunch and play at the restaurant's play structure. After barely touching her happy meal, Zoë was ready to go outside. Quickly taking off her shoes, she raced into the play area. Only one family was there. It was a Chinese mother and her three children (two girls and a boy). The boy was not yet walking, and the girls ranged in age from four to six. As my daughter and the two girls warily negotiated play in the ball pit, I didn't think much of it. My daughter was outgoing, and I had seen her handle similar situations easily.

Soon the sisters climbed into the brightly colored opaque tubes and stationed themselves at the control tower. The control tower was the highest point in the tube structure and contained windows and the only steering wheel. All the children in the tubes had to pass through this center to enter and exit the structure. Tiring of playing alone, it wasn't long before Zoë disappeared into the opaque tubes and up to the control tower. My mind began to wander, and Zoë's voice drew me back. It sounded as if she said, "I'm not fat."

Suddenly she was out of the tubes, crying. Through her tears, she informed me that the girls would not play with her or let her play with the steering wheel. It was near her nap time, so instead of sending her back into the play structure, I thought it best to head home. We started the long process of putting on her shoes and talking about why some children have a hard time sharing and taking turns. But this usually calming approach did not work. Zoë did not stop crying. Instead, her tears intensified. Attributing her inconsolable condition to tiredness, I tried to reassure her and hurried up the shoe process.

It was then, with her left arm extended toward me and her right hand pointing to her left arm, that she blurted out: "They said I couldn't play with them because I'm black! I'm not black. I AM NOT BLACK! I'm brown. I AM BROWN!" She began to cry, a shoulder-shaking, body-trembling cry. I quickly looked for the girls and, most importantly, for their mother. But, sometime in the midst of our conversation, the two girls had exited the tubes and the family had left. It was just my daughter and I, her sobbing and my alternating waves of anger, guilt, sadness, and powerlessness.

My three-year-old daughter had just been introduced to her place within the racialized gender hierarchy, and I had not been able to intervene . . . to protect her . . . to make it right. Zoë's age, gender, and race and the fact that she was alone made her appear an easy target for young girls experimenting with their own power. Had an older Black girl or younger White boy climbed into those tubes, I'm certain a different interaction would have occurred and, hence, a different outcome. In other words, though the words had been explicitly racial, the incident commingled race, gender, and age.

As a Black mother, I had always known that this would happen. Mistakenly, I had thought we would not have to tackle these issues until kindergarten. Standing in that playground, mother and daughter became one. We were both Black females and, as a result, despite her incredibly short history and my somewhat extensive experience, had been attacked at our core.

I begin this book at this place because the organization studied herein resembles that McDonald's play structure. Like the tubes, it was constructed as a safe place and contained both visible and hidden spaces for women and girls to flex their own power. Like the incident, oppressive whispers and resistant shouts punctuated the environment. I also begin here because it is from my personal history and experiences as a Black woman, girl, mother, daughter, sister, wife, and friend, as well as my academic training as a sociologist and an African American scholar, that this story is told.

Acknowledgments

An often-quoted African proverb states, "It takes a whole village to raise a child." Well, it took a whole village to deliver this book! I owe the completion of this project to many people who knowingly and unknowingly contributed to the intellectual, emotional, and spiritual strength that I relied on during the life of this project. It is with sincere appreciation that I acknowledge those who generously shared their time; offered information; read and commented on drafts; insisted that I continue; insisted that I take a break; walked with me; steamed with me; sat with me; held me; challenged my ideas; listened to my frustrations; and extended love, generosity, and the occasional kick in the pants.

First and foremost, I extend deep gratitude to the women and girls of the Girls Empowerment Project (GEP), whose dreams, fears, and amazing insights are the heart and soul of this project. I know that I have captured only a small portion of your creativity, strength, and wisdom in these pages. You all were the greatest source of inspiration.

I have been blessed with amazing friends and colleagues who supported me in many ways during the various stages of completing this project: Vicki Abadesco, Mary Grace Almandrez, Maxine Leeds Craig, Pam Dunn, Cheryl Finley, Marya Grambs, Breanne Harris; Jumoke Hinton-Hodge, Amy Joseph, Jerusalem Makonnen, Noa Mohablane, Vijaya Nagarajan; Jerry Neale, Pamela Balls-Organista, Dana Pepp, Judy Romero, Joe Sadusky, Joseph Savage, Ronald Sundstrum, Annick Wibben, Shawan Worsley, and the USF Writing Warriors. You all were there when life seemed to push me away from this goal. Thanks for watching the girls, cheering me on, reading drafts, refusing to leave the writing retreat until I finished, transcribing interviews, suggesting books, and just reminding me I could do it. You provided the needed support for me to "let go" and to let the book have a life of its own.

As this project began as a dissertation, thanks go to Jennifer Bair, Josh Gamson, and Paul Gilroy, my dissertation committee. Thanks for not giving up on me as I took a rather "nontraditional" path through the program. A special thanks to the Sociology Department at the University of San Francisco. Thanks for showing me that an academic community can be fun, inspiring, concerned about real-world issues, and intellectually engaging.

I would also like to acknowledge Diane Ganeles, Andrew Kenyon and Larin McLaughlin at State University of New York (SUNY) Press. Thank you for believing in my work and allowing me the time to get it done. I also gratefully acknowledge the anonymous reviewers whose questions, suggestions, and critical feedback pushed me to go farther and contributed to the final product.

Funding from Yale University's Dissertation Fellowship program and the Irvine Dissertation Fellows Program made the early part of this project possible. In addition, I gratefully acknowledge the financial support of the University of San Francisco's Faculty Development Fund. Funding from this program allowed me to complete the book.

Last, but certainly not least, much love and thanks go to my family. To my grandma, who passed away before I could finish, thanks for instilling in me the ability to dream, and the confidence to believe and pursue my dreams. Thanks also go to Anthony Baker for sharing so much of our time together with this project. Finally, I am forever grateful to my two daughters, Zoë and Asha. When I wanted to stop, I always heard your voices cheering, "Go Mama, Go!" It is for you, and for the little Black girl that still resides in me, that I dared to do this project.

Introduction

It was time for the next act to begin. On this bright and breezy Saturday afternoon in June, over 100 Sun Valley residents patiently waited to watch and participate in the Girls Empowerment Project's Community Talent Show.[1] Opened in 1993, the Girls Empowerment Project (hereafter GEP) was a single-sex, after-school program that served Black girls living in and around Sun Valley, the largest public housing development in Bay City. The talent show was part of a larger community event that included a health fair and a block party. It was the brainchild of the Nia Collective, a leadership and community service program for the older GEP girls. The girls of the Nia Collective had not only conceived of the idea of the community event but also coordinated and implemented it at every level. In sixteen-year-old Tangee's words, "We was the staff for this event."[2]

Onto the makeshift stage stepped three African American girls between the ages of four and six. Soon a crowd-pleasing hit blasted through the PA system. After the girls performed a few upbeat arm moves and turns, the first soloist began. She was the youngest of the dancing trio. While her partners moved to the back and assumed the side-to-side step-together rhythm and motion, she quickly moved to the front of the stage and began to do the butterfly. Back bent with her hands to her knees, she deftly rotated her hips, accentuating the move so that her torso and behind gyrated and popped in time to the music. She was good—perfectly imitating popular dance moves performed by women on music videos. Her mother jumped up and yelled, "You'd better shake it, girl!" Other members of the audience also joined in cheering her on. Drawing upon their encouragement, she turned her back to the audience. Looking over her shoulder, her almond eyes and coffee-colored face radiating joy, she gyrated and popped with more energy and enthusiasm. The audience, in particular her mother and a group of rowdy young men gathered at the back, rose to their feet and cheered her on. GEP staff members—the adult sponsors of the event—were silent.

1

Off to the side of the center stage, Ife, GEP's executive director, approached Tangee and Kisha, the GEP girls serving as the emcees for the event. According to Tangee, "Ife was mad and wanted to know why those girls were up there dancing like that?" Tangee remembered Ife saying, "Their mommas are not going to appreciate what their kids are up here doing." Kisha told Ife, "You can't get mad. Look what they get it from—TV, and you can't blame that. And if their momma let them do it then you can't say nothing about that. Well, you do get your opinion, but you can't do any-thing about it." Tangee chimed in, "You all don't want them to dance how they know how to dance, you just want them to do little African dances and stuff. People ain't going to do that when they trying to win a prize." The final words, however, belonged to Ife: "Shut up! Just, shut up! Don't say another word!"

When the performance ended, Ife took the microphone from Tangee and stepped on stage. In a voice laced with anger and frustration, she told the crowd, "This performance *does not* represent GEP! I wish that all the energy you've put into this dance, you put into these girls reading." The energy shifted, and tension filled the air. One member of the crowd loudly remarked, "She's doing too much." Others shouted out, "She's weak," "She ain't nobody." Some of the audience dispersed. The show never recovered. The block party never happened.

When I listened to the girls describe this event, I had two immediate but contradictory responses. The first was as a mother of two African American girls, and that reaction was very similar to that of GEP's staff. It went some-thing like this: "What were those girls doing up there? They shouldn't be up there poppin' their butts like that." My second response, my sociological mind interested in women's and girls' resistance, first just thought about the power of "da butt" and the booty dance. As bell hooks (1992) and Patricia Collins (2004) remind us, going all the way back to Sarah Bartmann, the Hottentot Venus, to Josephine Baker and coming into the present with Bey-once and all her bootylisciousness, "da butt," which is constructed in our imagination as an icon for sexuality, more specifically for sexual availability and promiscuity, has become so linked with the Black female body that I wondered about the possibility of Black women and girls experiencing them-selves—ourselves—outside of this box. I began to wonder about dance, with its explicit links to sex, sexuality, and desire, as a space wherein Black women and girls could challenge the dominant maps of meaning encircling our bodies. I also began to think about how we might navigate such repre-sentations within an organization such as GEP that was dedicated to Black female empowerment.

Polhemus (1993) writes that, "dance—the distillation of culture into its most metaphysical form—always embodies and identifies the gender-generated division of cultural realities" (11). Dance is charged precisely because of its connection to normative notions of gender and sexuality, which are key sites around which privilege and inequality are created and maintained. For women and girls, gendered sexual oppression is reflected in the Madonna/Whore dichotomy and within the United States due to the intersection of racist ideology with the good/bad woman construct—Black women and girls exist within a racialized sex/gender hierarchy where their bodies have been marked as unattractive, sexually deviant, and out of control. Dance provides a window into a community's and perhaps even a nation's sexual politics: those "ideas and social practices shaped by gender, race, and sexuality that frame all men and women's treatment of one another as well as how individual men and women are perceived and treated by others" (Collins 2004, 6).

Exploring how Black women and girls struggle with and against each other to resist stereotypes, imagine their identities, and move their bodies in a sociopolitical context that commodifies, objectifies, and devalues them has addressed issues raised in both academic and activist circles. For example, girls studies scholars have called for the creation of spaces where women and girls can form alliances to enable girls to "imagine what could be" outside of limiting race and gender narratives (Anyon 1983). Yet while the research on girls, girl power, and girl cultures has increased dramatically over the past ten years, few studies have examined the multigenerational dynamics between women and girls that can both limit and foster girls' rejection of hypersexualized and objectified representations of womanhood. In addition, few studies focus on the organizations in which their multigenerational work occurs.

Within *Imagining Black Womanhood*, I examine how Black women and girls work to change how they perceive and identify themselves, as well as how larger society views them within the context of an Africentric womanist after-school program. Specifically, I explore how GEP's organizational context mediated stereotypes of Black womanhood and structured how women and girls worked with and against each other to imagine and construct authentic and respectable Black femininities. Established in 1993, this single sex, after-school program was created to serve Black girls living in one of Bay City's largest, most impoverished, and isolated public housing developments. A self-proclaimed "Africentric" womanist program, GEP sought to challenge race and gender discourses that limited the lives of Black girls and to support them on the road to success.[3] Yet empowerment did not proceed as expected within this organization. Instead of a multigenerational alliance, the women and girls often appeared to struggle against each other. That is, class and generational differences, often made visible via public dance performances such as the community talent show, created conflicts that at times paralyzed the organization and made empowerment seem illusive.

Throughout *Imagining Black Womanhood*, I explore how women's and girls' identity work was shaped by, what I term, the *organizational power matrix*. Within this matrix, organizational culture, structure, and environment intersect and create sites of power that can be accessed and mobilized by organizational participants. In this way, women's and girls' ability to negotiate power and to ultimately imagine and negotiate Black femininities was concretely connected to their ability to access organizational power. For example, GEP women drew upon the cultural resources provided by the organization's Africentric womanist ideology and their position as staff to construct a hierarchy of Black femininities structured around self-definition, self-reliance, and sexual agency. This hierarchy, however, silenced and subordinated other Black femininities. GEP girls, drawing upon the organizational discourse of youth power and their power as consumers, challenged the staff's Africentric womanist femininity and asserted the right to be recognized not for "how we are like you" but for "how we are." The key site of this negotiation between Africentric womanist femininity and the girls' own "decent girl" femininity, between respectability and respect, was dance. This dual focus on the organization and the multigenerational aspect of women's and girls' identity work addresses gaps found within sociology and the multidisciplinary girls' studies literature on girls' culture, and resistance. The evidence from this case captures the importance of the organizational power matrix in delineating the processes by which women and girls negotiate identity and power and provides theoretical insight into the relationship among power, identity work, and organizational context.

IDENTITY WORK

In April 2007, during the airing of MSNBC's *Imus in the Morning*, host Don Imus and Bernard McGuirk, the show's executive producer, engaged in lively banter about the 2007 NCAA women's basketball championship finals between Rutgers and Tennessee. Imus, noting the tattoos etched on the bodies of the Rutgers team, described the young women as "rough girls." McGuirk remarked that the team, composed of eight African American and two Caucasian players, included "some hard-core hos." Imus followed, "That's some nappy-headed hos there."[4]

Immediately following his comments, Black Americans called for Imus to be fired for his dehumanizing racist and sexist remarks. Amid protests and sponsor pullouts, Imus was suspended and eventually terminated. Yet the Imus controversy did more than open up old wounds regarding White male denigration of Black womanhood. It also forced African Americans to look at the proliferation of such images within its own quarters. In response to Imus's comments and their aftermath, Oprah Winfrey hosted a two-day forum.[5] What was made clear during the two-day event, and in many conversations happening in kitchens, classrooms, offices, and online blogs, was that mainstream media, often interpreted by African Americans as White, were not solely responsible for the dehumanization of the Rutgers women and, by extension, Black women and girls at large. Though these hypersexualized representations of Black womanhood did not originate with rap music, with the global rise of hip-hop culture images of Black women as "hos" have taken up home and become normalized within popular culture (hooks 1981; Gilman 1985; Collins 2004). Hip-hop, and in particular rap music, has troubled the easy line between Black and White, between victims and villains, between Us and Them. Imus's remarks forced African Americans to come to terms with ways that "the madness visited upon hip-hop generation women comes as much from within their own communities as from without" (Sharpley-Whiting 2007, 11).[6]

Researchers suggest that during early adolescence, girls become both capable of and thus "vulnerable to internalizing the impossible ideals and images" of idealized or conventional femininity (Debold, as quoted in Brown 1998, 7). Though unmarked, idealized femininity, or what Connell (1987) would call emphasized femininity, is tied to White, middle-class, heterosexual womanhood and constructed around notions of passivity, silence, subordination, selflessness, and purity. While already familiar with the image, adolescent girls come to understand the implications of such images for their own lives as girls and future women.[7]

Scholars have found that it can be especially difficult for Black girls to grapple with constructions of womanhood (Ladner 1972; Fordham 1993; Fine and Zane 1995). Of particular note is the way in which Black girls are at once invisible and hypervisible in popular culture. Within the United States the norm for physical beauty is whiteness. As a result, Black girls are rarely featured in popular media and are less visible than their White counterparts. When Black girls are present, however, they are often cast as undesirable, unlikable, and hypersexual. For example, consider the following episode from the popular Disney television series, "Hannah Montana." In the episode "I Can't Make You Love Hannah If You Don't," a two-part tale of girlhood, race, and sexuality unfolds.[8] In the first story line, Hannah Montana (Miley Cyrus's stage name in real life and on the show) finds out that her new boyfriend, Jason, doesn't like Hannah Montana. In a series of moves, Miley attempts to change Hannah and does things on stage that Jason suggested would "make her cooler." In the end, though Miley fails to get Jason to like Hannah, her friends and father comfort her with the message that she will find someone that likes her for who she is.

In the second story line, a different type of girl is presented. This story line features Olivia, a young African American girl. Olivia emerges from the beach and bumps into Jackson, Miley's brother. Her presence is unusual, as the cast is predominately White, except for the occasional appearance by Roxy, Hannah Montana's overprotective bodyguard; Amber, the local mean girl; and Cooper, Jackson's best friend. Almost immediately, Olivia, described as a "party-type," shows an interest in Jackson.[9] Jackson is interested in Olivia as well, until he learns that she is Cooper's sister. But "Olivia won't take no for an answer" and kisses Jackson.[10] Cooper walks in just in time to witness this exchange. As expected, Cooper is upset. Olivia lies and claims that he was "all over" me. Believing his sister, Cooper opens the door to leave and follow his sister home, only to find Olivia kissing the pizza delivery boy. Shocked, Cooper forgives Jackson.

Within this episode, Miley and Olivia make explicit the hegemonic discourses or "our commonsense" understanding concerning girlhood, race, and sexuality. Miley's character, despite having an "official" date and "beau," attempts to please her man while maintaining her sexual purity. In stark contrast, Olivia is heavily sexualized, making out with boys she barely knows. The two story lines work together to construct White girls as innocent and cute and Black girls as sexual, untrustworthy, and out of control. In other words, within mainstream popular culture, the "powerful Western image of girlhood innocence and passive sexuality that prevails for white girls" is displaced by the image of African American girls as sexual beings (Ferguson 2000, 84). Black girls must confront images of themselves as "hos"—party girls, sexually available teens, hypersexualized dancers, and teen mothers. Black girls, as well as those around them, learn early on that Black womanhood is a devalued position.

Although representations do not determine behavior, they do provide social scripts that suggest how to "do femininity." Collins (2004) argues that such images are controlling images that justify oppression and "manufacture consent, so that we often collude in our own subordination" (50). Researchers have found that frequent exposure to sexualized images of Black womanhood, such as those found within popular culture, and specifically music videos, contributes to Black girls' higher acceptance of hegemonic ideologies regarding the sexual objectification of women and more traditional gender role attitudes (Ward 2002). In addition, this exposure contributes to more accepting attitudes toward sexual harassment (Strouse, Goodwin, and Roscoe 1994), higher frequency of STDs, alcohol and drug abuse, multiple sex partners (MEE 2005), and teen dating violence (Johnson et al. 1995). The constant repetition of such representations reifies "stereotypical gender schema, which influence subsequent social judgments and impressions . . . with the greater likelihood that they will be used to guide behavior" (Ward, Hansbrough, and Walker 2005). Given the high amounts of media consumption by African Americans and the more sexually explicit content found in their viewing habits, concern regarding young black women's identity options is warranted.[11]

Stevens (2002) found that due to the need to "enhance self-efficacy capacities in the face of socially denigrating experiences," Black girls engage in "identity exploration earlier than white (majority) teens" (25). She suggests that Black girls develop "skilled, unique, expressive, and assertive styles of relating as a way to negotiate [a] perceived hostile environment and to resist the controlling racist definitions of them" (61). Similarly, Ward (1990) notes the following:

> The process of being and becoming black provides young women . . . an opportunity for role negation—the repudiation of both race- and gender-based stereotypes [as well as] . . . an opportunity to create a new and personally defined identity on one's own terms. (228)

Black girls must engage in *identity work*.

Identity work is both an individual and a collective task. On the individual level, it refers to the "range of activities individuals engage in to create, present and sustain personal identities that are congruent with and supportive of their self concept" (Snow and Anderson 1987, 1348). Identity work contains an understanding of identities as socially constructed phenomena that represent our positioning within the social hierarchy. In other words, identities are not an essence waiting to be discovered. Rather, identity itself is best understood as a form of work, a "production which is never complete, always in process, and always constituted within, not outside, representation" (Hall 1990, 222). The use of the concept of identity work reminds us that, even at the individual level, identity is an accomplishment.

At the group level, Ponse (1978) suggests that identity work is the "techniques, strategies and methods that have as their purpose effecting a change in the meaning of a particular identity or a change in the identity itself" (199). Drawing upon the experiences of lesbians, Ponse suggests that identity work is implemented by "providing role models of proud gays, explanatory rationales and positive interpretations of gayness, accounts of other gay people's experiences, as well as the opportunity for the novice to talk about her own experience of lesbianism" (106). Key to identity work is the two-way push for change: Identity workers seek to change both how individuals perceive and identify themselves, as well as how larger society views the collective group. In many cases, the outcome of identity work is the creation of a shared community and, in some cases, a politicized collective identity.

Identity work has been a central component of Black women's activism. Beginning in the latter part of the nineteenth century, Black women came together in churches and clubs to "uplift the race." Possessing an understanding of the relationship between representations and social power, these "race women" set about redefining and representing themselves in an effort to secure their rights. In particular, they took on the mantle of respectability to challenge the racist and sexist stereotypes that defined Black women as lazy, loose, and licentious, and thus outside of "true" womanhood (Higginbotham 1993; Carby 1997; White 2001).

While the definition of respectability varies across time and place, during this period it contained several core themes: temperance, thrift, industriousness, cleanliness, refined manners, and Victorian sexual morals. Black women challenged their placement outside of respectability because to be defined as outside of the cult of "true" womanhood maintained and justified their continued economic and sexual exploitation. Therefore, Black women sought the protection that being "inside" could afford. To counter these negative images and lack of protection, Black women employed a "politics of respectability"; a racialized gender strategy that both condemned America's racial state and challenged what they perceived as negative patterns and attitudes within the Black world (Higginbotham 1993). Under the rubric of respectability, Black women utilized three tactics: First, they publicly protested their unequal treatment and worsening condition. Second, using their own bodies, they introduced alternative images of Black womanhood to challenge the negative images surrounding them. Finally, they challenged what they perceived as negative patterns and attitudes within the Black community (Higginbotham 1993; Carby 1997; White 2001).

Research on Black women's activism during the club movement has significantly contributed to scholarship on identity work and highlights three important points: First, scholars make clear that while the social order is shaped by dominant society, domination is never absolute (Giddings 1984; Higginbotham 1993; White 2001). Rather, as Foucault (1980) argued, "There are no relations of power without resistances; the latter are all the more real and effective because they are formed right at the point where relations of power are exercised (142). Within this framework, Black women and girls are not powerless—they are agents that recreate, resist, and reshape the social terrain. For example, as part of their politics of respectability, elite middle-class and working-poor Black women "boldly asserted the will and agency to define themselves outside the parameters of prevailing racist discourse" (Higginbotham 1993, 192). Moreover, Black women did not simply imitate the respectability discourse in circulation, as put forth by White women's groups. Rather, they reconstructed "respectable" to fit them. That is, while respectable White women were constrained by the cult of domesticity and urged to avoid the public sphere, Black women defined respectable as being active in the fight for racial equality as well as active in the labor market (White 2001, 36).

Second, the research on Black women's politics of respectability illustrates that identity work occurs on two levels: between dominant and marginalized groups, and among members of marginalized groups (Higginbotham 1993; Carby 1997; White 2001). For example, the same politics that empowered club and churchwomen also set into motion the self-regulation of one's own behavior as well as that of other Blacks. As a result, the policing and disciplining of Black women's behavior in cities was not just the domain of White agencies and institutions but also a "perception of Black institutions and organizations and the Black middle class" (Carby 1997, 153). Unfortunately, by censuring themselves and other Blacks who did not behave in a "respectable" manner, these women unintentionally supported the stereotypes they were attempting to dismantle (White 2001). That is, by adopting this position, they failed to challenge the inherently racist, sexist, and classist assumptions that served as the foundation of the respectability discourse. Moreover, by disciplining the bodies of working-class women, middle-class Black women ensured their own class privilege (Higginbotham 1993; Carby 1997; White 2001). Black femininities or representations of Black womanhood became stratified and reflected the class, regional, and generational power differentials among Black women. Thus identity work research must attend to the relationships of power both between and among dominant and subordinate groups.

Finally, research on Black women's respectability politics illustrates that Black women's empowerment does not happen "out there" but, rather, within particular social spaces such as clubs and churches. Collins (1991) notes:

> While domination may be inevitable as a social fact, it is unlikely to be hegemonic as an ideology within that social space where Black women speak freely. . . . By advancing Black women's empowerment through self-definition, the safe spaces housing this culture of resistance help Black women resist the dominant ideology promulgated not only outside Black communities but within African American institutions. (95)

Researchers exploring the identity work strategies of nineteenth-century church and club women agree that the construction of "safe spaces" was vital to the development of Black women's self-definition and politics of respectability. The churches and clubs provided a space wherein Black women could question and challenge hegemonic ideologies. How these organizations shape and shift identity work, however, is left relatively unexplored. Yet given that race and gender are socially constructed, and that their patterns of power and oppression vary across time and place, it is imperative to position identity work within specific organizational contexts. Thus this research points to the importance of within-group power dynamics and organizational context as key factors in understanding Black women's and girls' negotiation of power and hence identity.

IDENTITY WORK AND ORGANIZATIONAL CONTEXT

Social movement scholars have used the concept of free space to describe places conducive for constructing cultures of resistance and challenging oppression. Evans and Boyte (1986) write:

> Free spaces are the environments in which people are able to learn a new self-respect, a deeper and more assertive group identity, public skills, and values of cooperation and civic virtue. Put simply, free spaces are settings between private lives and large-scale institutions where ordinary citizens can act with dignity, independence, and vision. (17–18)

Free spaces are critical sites in the process of democracy and serve as the basis for constructing a culture of resistance. The concept of free space speaks directly to those safe spaces described by Collins (1991) as key in supporting Black women's empowerment.

Researchers also have noted the complicated power relationships that may exist within such "free" or "safe spaces." Evans and Boyte (1986) note:

> Free spaces are never pure phenomenon. In the real world, they are always complex, shifting, and dynamic—partial in their freedom and democratic participation, marked by parochialism of class, gender, race, and other biases of the groups which maintain them. (19)

In other words, while free spaces may offer space for marginalized groups to "act with dignity, independence, and vision," such spaces may not be free to all members within a group. To fully grasp the contours of "free spaces," careful attention must be paid to the power dynamics and internal fractures within groups. Moreover, since free spaces are often located within organizational sites that have their own logic and processes, attention to the organizational aspects of such spaces is necessary.

CONCEPTUALIZING THE ORGANIZATIONAL POWER MATRIX

Organizations are social and symbolic arenas where new relations, new representations, and new knowledge can be formed, sometimes against, sometimes tangential to, and sometimes coinciding with the interests of those holding power (Levinson and Holland 1996). They mediate between macro-structural forces and individuals (Connell 1987; Collins 1998) and influence what and how we think, as well as mobilize us for action (Katzenstein 1990; Fried 1994). As such, they provide key information about identity production processes.

Scholars have identified three organizational domains that shape and structure organizational power dynamics: organizational environment, organizational culture, and organizational structure. Organizational environment is characterized by the key material and ideological milieus that impact upon an organization's creation, survival, and success (DiMaggio and Powell 1991[1983]; Fried 1994; Bordt 1997). It addresses the role of extra-organizational processes and demands on an organization's internal functioning, structure, and goals. Scholars have found that an organization's resource dependencies and institutional context can influence an organization's mission, goals, structure, and success (DiMaggio and Powell 1991[1983]; Milofsky and Romo 1988; Gamson 1996).[12] Moreover, as a result of nonprofit organizations' dependency on external funding, the distinction between resource dependency and institutional factors is often blurred, because both the nonprofit and its funding organizations are located within an institutional context that "mirrors and incorporates the larger social structure of which they are a part" (Powell and Friedkin 1987, 181). Thus for nonprofit organizations such as GEP, it is often difficult to disentangle resource dependency and institutional influence on organizational culture or structure. Ultimately, an organization's environment, by censuring political action, shifting an organizations' mission, and restricting funds to hierarchically or bureaucratically structured organizations, simultaneously provides constraints and opportunities that can impact upon the identity work that occurs within and by an organization. It shapes who has power and voice, which race, class, and gender projects will be articulated, and how such constructions will be negotiated.

Organizational culture refers to the collective understanding and norms often expressed through symbols, rituals, ideologies, and language (Fried 1994). As with all forms of culture, this is not a static process but is part of an ongoing process carried out by actors and agents both limited and facilitated by the organization. That is, while environmental factors as well as the founders have a lasting impact on an organization, organizational culture is a continual process not of reproduction but of production. Though embedded within the larger sociopolitical context, and oftentimes shifting in response to resource dependencies, organizational culture also has the capacity to shape resource relationships, organizational structure, and people's ideas and ideologies. Thus similar to the previous finding on organizational environment, the relationship between organizational culture and environment is interactive and dynamic.

Finally, organizational structure delineates how power is formally structured to move within an organization, and it serves as the foundation for decision-making processes and procedures (Tayeb 1988). The connection between organizational structure and organizational power relations is clear: Those with the ability to influence and make decisions have power. However, while the organizational structure constrains our interactions, it is not a rigid, unchanging feature of organizations (Hall 1987). Participants modify the structure, and organizational culture can override formal structural procedures and models. Informal structures, shaped by the organizational culture and environment, may change and transform the formal power structure in place. In addition, organizational culture can dictate organizational structure, as in the case of second-wave feminist organizations. Thus it is not enough to focus on one organizational arena as the sole site or domain of power. These domains interact and influence each other. As a result, an organizational analysis that takes into account these interacting domains is needed to adequately understand identity work.

In this work I propose the term *organizational power matrix* to refer to the configuration of power relationships within an organization and to address the theoretical shortcomings found within research on identity work. Within this framework, organizational culture, structure, and environment are conceptualized as ideological, positional, and material domains of power that intersect and shape the who, the what, and the how of identity work. In this way, these domains serve as resources that organizational actors mobilize in pursuit of their goals and, in this case, identity work. Most important, this organizational power matrix may or may not conform to macro-relations of power. That is, I am suggesting that while poor Black girls may be identified as oppressed along race, class, gender, age, and sexuality lines, this experience of oppression may be challenged within particular organizational spaces—that organizations, while clearly embedded within larger societal structures of power, do not merely replicate or reproduce these relations. A careful examination of the relationship among an organization's environment, culture, and structure is needed to ascertain how these features facilitate the internal movement of power and, consequently, the business of identity work within such spaces.

CHAPTER OUTLINE

Exploring how Black women and girls create viable cultural identities and negotiate power within specific organizational sites furthers our theoretical endeavors to understand how power and privilege are reproduced within societies. To this end, chapter 1 introduces the Girls Empowerment Project and my role(s) as a participant observer and researcher. I examine in chapter 2 GEP's organizational environment—one element of the power matrix. I suggest that GEP's organizational environment, composed of both the sociopolitical and institutional contexts that impacted upon the organization's emergence and development, was defined by the "teen pregnancy epidemic" of the 1980s and early 1990s and represented by the figure of "The Urban Girl." During this moment, the nation's collective anxieties regarding shifting sexual trends and economic dislocations were understood to be caused by teen pregnancy and blamed on "The Urban Girl." As a result, both dominant and indigenous group members sought to control the sexuality, reproduction, and "dependency" of poor Black girls. Moreover, GEP's institutional context—that area defined by GEP's identity as a nonprofit service organization linked to other organizations through resource opportunities and dependencies—supported this discourse of control. That is, in a period of shrinking economic opportunities and increased competition within the nonprofit sector, both governmental and philanthropic organizations concentrated funds targeting economic self-sufficiency and strengthening the "inner city," thereby encouraging and supporting the growth and development of programs such as GEP.

I examine in chapter 3 GEP's culture of empowerment, paying particular attention to the organization's founding and revised mission statements. I suggest that GEP's founders drew upon the race, class, and gender reforms of the period to develop a culturally relevant, single-sex, after-school program for Black girls living in public housing. In the process, they developed an organizational ideology that supported equal access and individual empowerment and a separate and safe space for marginalized group members. Grounded in these discourses, GEP developed an organizational culture of empowerment that utilized a "Black-female-only safe space" and consciousness-raising as strategies to assist girls in overcoming structural barriers and social factors such as negative stereotyping, poverty, and limited educational opportunities to achieve success. Though problematic in its articulation of power as well as in its representation of Black girlhood, this culture of empowerment laid the ideological foundation necessary for GEP women and girls to reshape GEP into a "homeplace" where they could critique, imagine, and recreate representations of girlhood and womanhood.

Chapter 4 details GEP's organizational structure and the resulting organizational power matrix. I demonstrate that, structurally, GEP developed into an organization that contained both bureaucratic and collective elements. As a result, it had ambiguous power relations that fostered the development of an organizational space that altered the terrain of power and voice that the staff and girls experienced in their daily-lived experiences. In other words, GEP's structure created power relations that differed from those present in the macro-structural context and opened up space for both women and girls to "do" power. Girls and women spoke up, spoke out, walked in, and walked out within the context of GEP—they learned strategies and experienced opportunities to consciously and unconsciously wield power. This alteration of power relations laid the foundation for the identity work that occurred within the organization.

Having sketched a detailed picture of GEP's organizational power matrix, in chapters 5 and 6 I explore how GEP women and girls moved with and against each other to negotiate and construct Black femininities. In chapter 5, I excavate GEP's women's collective racialized gender regime. While it was true that GEP women were highly influenced by organizational ideologies and structures, they were not passive agents in this process. GEP women built upon their personal experiences as well as GEP's organizational discourse and practice to construct an Africentric womanist femininity that ranked Black femininities along three dimensions: (1) self-definition, (2) self-reliance, and (3) sexual agency. This hierarchy of Black femininities simultaneously centered and marginalized, included and excluded. It differently empowered and rewarded women and girls within GEP. However, GEP girls had their own decent girl femininity that both mapped onto and challenged GEP's Africentric womanist femininity. GEP girls' empowerment often took the form of challenging staff's Africentric womanist respectability with a politics of respect. GEP girls' "politics of respect" pushed for a recognition of self, not "how I am like you, or "how you want me to be" but, rather, "as I am."

Chapter 6 examines GEP's dance politics, the key site of negotiation between the girls' politics of respect and the staff's politics of respectability. Dance often served as a public performance of GEP's identity work. Consequently, dance performances were fraught with tension and heavily monitored to ensure an "appropriate" public display of Black femininity. From a place of respect, GEP girls insisted on popular dance and resisted staff-supported African dance. Through this process of insistence and resistance, they redefined and empowered themselves as urban Black girls with their own unique and important history and identities that must be recognized.

I conclude this book with a review of the theoretical challenges this research poses to the existing literature on identity work, empowerment, and Black women's and girls' sexual politics. I address the importance of organizational context for furthering our understanding of the ways in which multiclass, multigenerational groups negotiate power and identity in particular and for theorizing and conceptualizing power, identity work, and empowerment in general.

1

Girls Empowerment Project

The potential of places like GEP . . . starting from when you're a child, when you know that there are successful Black women . . . that we contributed so much . . . and not only that that we're beautiful—that it's alright for us to be different shapes and shades and our hair to be different textures. And that's not what this society teaches. But if you have places like GEP where you see that, constantly see that and it's not in a negative light or it's not in something someone made up on television but it is something that is real. That's showing much love to me. . . . Places like GEP are necessary, definitely necessary, to excise white supremacy. Definitely necessary! . . . If I had GEP when I was that age, Lord have Mercy, I don't know where I would be right now. (Aisha, age twenty-four, program coordinator)

Recognizing the daily assaults on Black girls, GEP was created to be a place where girls and staff could challenge and confront representations and practices that limited and degraded the aspirations and lives of low-income Black girls. It was designed to be a social space where women and girls could work on themselves outside the "gaze" of dominant and indigenous groups and "go about the business of fashioning themselves" (O'Neale 1986, 139, as quoted in Collins 1991, 95). In this chapter, I describe GEP and the community in which it was located. I also detail my own involvement with the organization and the research process.

In the spring of 1991, Melinda George, the cofounder of Bay City's Women's Building and the city's first battered women's shelter, created the Girls Leadership Project. At this time Melinda, a well-known White feminist organizer and successful nonprofit program developer within Bay City's women's and philanthropic communities, secured a $50,000 planning grant to investigate the needs as well as resources available in Bay City for girls. In this formative stage, Melinda teamed up with Chris, an African American community activist known for representing the interests of low-income public housing residents. During this initial period, both women met with staff at numerous public and private agencies to ascertain what services were available as well as what was needed for girls. They also interviewed fifty-five girls to get their perspectives on what kinds of programming they liked and wanted (GEP 1992b, 7).

As part of this phase, the two women created an interim steering committee composed of a diverse group of community leaders, activists, youth workers, educators, social service providers, and public housing residents, who began to formulate plans for a leadership and self-esteem program for low-income girls. I was a part of this committee. We wrote:

> We, the Girls Leadership Project, are developing a program for girls designed to attract and reach girls where they are, and provide leadership, self-esteem, empowerment, and economic development skills. It will be located on-site in a public housing development in Bay City and shaped by girls themselves, by women who work with girls, and by residents of the community. Because of the demographics of who is poor and at the highest risk in the city, the first program will be targeted primarily to African American girls and developed within a context of Afrocentric cultural values. (Women's Building 1992)

This committee, composed of eight African American women and two White women, eventually became GEP's Executive Management Committee. Over nine months, we met to create the Girls Empowerment Program (GEP): "A Program for Inner City Mothers of Tomorrow" (GEP 1992b, 1). It is hard to describe the excitement I felt as we worked to create GEP. I truly believed I was working to create deep change for and with women and girls I cared about. Once GEP opened, I transitioned into a member of the board of directors. In this role, I continued to work with other women to dream and envision an organization before heading off to graduate school.

GEP's first years were volatile. There were lawsuits, financial challenges, and struggles over space and the housing of the program, and within weeks of being hired, GEP's first executive director was let go. Despite these challenges, the program kept its promise to serve the girls of Sun Valley. At the time of this research, the agency had served at least 100 girls annually for thirteen years.[1]

SUN VALLEY

Living in Sun Valley is great, once you get used to it. The bad thing about Sun Valley is that there are too many gangsters. (Tenda, GEP girl age twelve)

My experience with Sun Valley and some of the people has been frightening and at times hectic. Nowadays you can't be hanging out late without the fear of getting shot, raped, and even kidnapped. These things happen everywhere, but in a neighborhood such as mine, it is almost expected to happen, because bad things have always happened. I usually cry myself to sleep knowing when I wake up I will still be in Sun Valley, in the projects, in the ghetto, as usual. (Tracy, GEP girl age sixteen)

Living in Sun Valley feels nice, and I feel kind of safe. Some people around my neighborhood treat me well. Other people don't say anything to me. When there are drive-bys or when someone has a knife or when there is fighting, I don't feel safe. I stay inside when these things are happening, because I feel uncomfortable. If I could change anything about Sun Valley, I would try to ask everyone to help clean our community. I would ask people to plant flowers and have butterflies flying around. (Nikki, GEP girl age eleven)

I don't like Sun Valley. It's dirty, stanky, messy, dookie. It's difficult seeing drunk people and stuff—people robbing people and stuff. (Diamond, GEP girl age twelve)

It isn't that bad living in Sun Valley, because there is lots of loving in Sun Valley. There are people that give support and love in Sun Valley. (Portia, GEP girl age eleven)

During the summer of 1993, GEP opened its doors in Sun Valley, the largest of the forty-eight public housing developments in Bay City. Descending the hill into Sun Valley was like entering another world. Housed on forty-nine acres and home to approximately 2,000 residents, Sun Valley contained over 750 units, as compared to other public housing developments in the city, which ranged from fifty to 250 units. Nestled in a valley, the development contrasted sharply with the surrounding cities' row houses and apartments. Strangely, there was a sense of space here, endlessness in the midst of intense crowding.

Sun Valley was developed in 1940 as "Whites-only" transitional housing for young, working-class families in the postwar economy.[2] By the 1950s, the development was integrated, albeit segregated. That is, Whites lived in one section, Latinos in another, and African Americans in yet another (Peacock 1999). Between the 1950s and the 1970s, many small businesses were located along Sun Valley Avenue, the main corridor running through the development. According to local residents, however, the 1960s brought great changes to this neighborhood. The shift from a manufacturing to a service economy resulted in massive economic dislocations. Whites moved out. A "rougher" crowd moved in, and "drugs and purse snatching" became more prevalent (Peacock 1999).[3] By the 1970s, small businesses had left the area due to robberies, fire, shoplifting, and vandalism.

Here in this urban landscape, race, class, and gender oppression converged, and they were often experienced as poverty, poor education, poor health, violence, and incarceration. For example, in 1993, the year GEP opened its doors, 46 percent of African American children lived in poverty or near poverty nationwide. Of this number, almost 10 percent lived in deep poverty, with family incomes 50 percent below the poverty line (Bennett 1995). These figures were mirrored within Bay City. For example, while only 10 percent of the city's overall population was African American, 64 percent of the youth residing in public housing were African American (SFHA 1992). In addition, Blacks in Bay City constituted 43.4 percent of the city's AFDC clients (SFDSS 1992).

Moreover, the growth of technology and internet industries in Silicon Valley further exacerbated the two-tiered labor divide in Bay City. These industries created a class of young professionals with large amounts of disposable income that transformed the economic and social character of Bay City. Between 1994 and 1996, the gap between the rich and the poor within Bay City increased by nearly 40 percent. This was the largest two-year increase in the twenty years covered by the survey (Zoll 1998). Housing prices soared, and many poor, working-class, and middle-class Black families were pushed out of their homes and into the streets or outside of Bay City to lower-rent, lower-mortgage communities. Between 1990 and 2000, Bay City's African American population dropped by 15 percent. This was the highest rate of decline found across the nation's fifty most populous cities (McCormick 2001). Many of those who did stay were residents of public housing that were too poor to move.

Adding to these economic realities, the triple impact of crack addiction, HIV infection, and imprisonment devastated many Black families. Children were orphaned and pushed into foster care systems, cared for by grandparents, or moved among various family members. According to *The New York Times*, at one urban middle school in Bay City, almost two-thirds of the students were newly orphaned, with 50 percent living with their grandparents (Navarro 1992). Many young people were forced to raise themselves, some joined "sets," and some sold crack to support themselves and their families. [4]

These were the realities of young girls in Sun Valley at the time that GEP was founded. During this period, Sun Valley was considered the most dangerous public housing development in Bay City. It had one of the highest rates of violence of any neighborhood in the city, averaging five to ten homicides a year (GEP 1992b). Most of the homicides and assaults were the result of drive-by shootings, characteristic of the crack trade. Throughout the neighborhood, abandoned cars dotted the parking lots. Trash lined the streets and covered the so-called "yards." The air was filled with dirt and debris whipped up by the strong winds and lack of plant life to hold the soil. Makeshift memorials dedicated to fallen homies, fathers, sons, and brothers sprinkled the landscape.

Between 1993 and 2000, however, Sun Valley experienced many changes. GEP's administrative director, a former resident of Sun Valley, remarked:

> I've seen Sun Valley go from the comfort zone in '67 to what they call the swamp, with no grass. It had drive-bys. It was not a good thing out here. I've seen the physical appearance go back to what it was in '67. I think some of it is the repercussions of what transpired in between the wars, the drive-bys, . . . the drug dealing . . . they have come a long way in cleaning the community, but I think it has left a scar, and I don't know if it will ever get back to where it was as a community, but it's getting better and I think a lot of it has to do with our girls. (Roxanne, age fifty-four)

Similarly, Kim, a resident of Sun Valley off and on for fourteen years, noted:

> There used to be a lot of shooting, and driving up on sidewalks when the twins was [sic] little. When they were babies they'd be running from cars up on the sidewalks, playgrounds, police chasing. Now since they got the Beijings (local slang for Housing Authority's private security force) it's calmed down a bit, it's even better. They started looking better. (mother of GEP girls, age thirty-five)

Finally, sixteen-year-old Tracy reflected:

> I see that Sun Valley has changed from a place where people were shooting bullets to a place where people are shooting out paint for the houses, grass for the lawns, and a remodeled home to live in. I like Sun Valley for these reasons and because it is a place where everyone knows each other. (GEP girl)

Sun Valley had indeed changed. The development's townhouses and apartments had been remodeled and given fresh coats of pastel paints. Grass covered what were once dirt yards. Sun Towers, a twenty-story twin tower structure that housed between 2,000 and 3,000 residents, was demolished and replaced by new low-income townhouses.

Most important, as both the adults and girls noted, the increase in both public and private security forces "calmed" Sun Valley "down a bit." During this period, a new police substation was placed inside an apartment located at the center of the development. In addition, Bay City's Housing Authority implemented a controversial housing policy that evicted residents who were themselves drug dealers or who harbored known drug dealers. They also hired, "The Beijings," a paramilitary-clad private security company to patrol the development. The result was that many of the young men, often the perpetrators and targets of the violence, were removed from the neighborhood via the new housing policy, incarceration, forced relocation for safety, and, in some cases, death.

Despite the decrease in violence, during the research period Sun Valley was still extremely impoverished and isolated from city services and other parts of the city. In 1998, the average household income within the development totaled approximately $9,000, with 65 percent of all the families receiving some form of public assistance (SFHA 1998). As of 2007, little had changed. For example, while Blacks comprised only 8 percent of the total population of Bay City, they represented 70 percent of the residents of Sun Valley. Within this community, women headed 90 percent of the households, and the average household income totaled approximately $12,726, with 65 percent of all the families receiving some form of public assistance (SFHA 2007). Public transportation service to and from this area remained poor; there were no large grocery stores, banks, or gas stations in the area. Only one gated and barred convenience store stood as a reminder of the small business community that once thrived along Sun Valley Avenue.

As a result of this isolation, the African American community within Sun Valley was very close-knit. Families appeared to know each other, or at least know of each other. Many were related, and those that were not were made family by adding "Auntie" or "play" in front of "sista," "cousin," or "mama." This enmeshment could be found in the many informal child care and transportation arrangements.[5] For example, Esther, a GEP parent honored at the organization's five-year anniversary celebration for her leadership and courage in shaping a better world, served as a community othermother who raised her own five children plus informally raised two nieces and four neighborhood girls. If you wanted to know what was going on in Sun Valley or with GEP girls, you asked Esther. Neighbors sought her out for advice and assistance, and she often referred both girls and their caregivers to GEP.

INSIDE GEP

Within the Sun Valley community, GEP had a strong and growing presence. When the organization first opened its doors, it shared a space inside the local Boys and Girls Club at the center of the housing development. During the research period, however, GEP had three locations within the Sun Valley community: the administrative office, the "Village" site, and the bungalow. GEP's administrative office was located along Sun Valley Avenue in one of the renovated townhouses. In many ways this office was the "adult space." The executive director and administrative director had offices at this location. Administrative business and weekly staff meetings took place within this structure. This was also where the parents and other adults of the community went for support. In 1998, GEP opened the village office, a satellite site within a community center that housed service providers for the displaced residents of the demolished Sun Towers. This site was home to the director of programs, the girls' advocate, and group C, the fifteen-to-eighteen-year-old girls who attended the program.

The heart of the program, however, was the small, light-blue bungalow located at the edge of the development. The bungalow was a single-story structure consisting of three "classrooms," a kitchen area and two bathrooms surrounded by a six-foot-high industrial-strength fence. As you entered the gated area, you were immediately aware of the garden. Maintained by girls, staff, and a dedicated core of volunteers, the garden featured cherry tomatoes, rosemary, lavender, strawberries, lemon grass, medicinal herbs, vegetables, and flowers. In the spring, it appeared as an oasis of life and beauty in the otherwise dusty, urban environment. Situated on a hill, the front of the bungalow looked down at row upon row of townhouses, while the back looked up and away from the community. Its physical location was symbolic: while this was a program for the young women of the community, it was not necessarily from or of this community but negotiated an uneasy tension between these worlds.

Once inside the bungalow, you knew you had entered a space for Black women and girls. Couches, pillows, and rugs dotted the interior, and the walls were covered with photos, posters, artwork, and poetry celebrating the legacy, creativity, and beauty of Black women and girls. Through the main door, you looked directly into the kitchen area, which contained a refrigerator, a sink, lots of cabinets, and a series of hotplates. To the left was the group B (twelve-to-fifteen-year-old girls) space. This area consisted of two rooms: the "chill-out" room, which was also home to the program's impressive library, and group B's work area. The walls in group B were lined with the program coordinator's desk, four computer work spaces, and a printer. On the back wall, above the couch, were seven human torso silhouettes akin to those used in gun target practice. Each torso was surrounded by the words "They're out to get me . . ."

Figure 1.1
They're Out to Get Me

They're out to get me	cuz I'm Black
They're out to get me	cuz I'm smart
They're out to get me	cuz I'm pretty
They're out to get me	cuz I'm female
They're out to get me	cuz I'm strong
They're out to get me	cuz I'm from the ghetto

The girls' statements, combined with the images, created a powerful impact. Something different was at work here, and it was this difference that was the spark and spirit of the organization.

Returning to the entry area, down the narrow hallway, and past the bathrooms was the group A area. Shaped like a rectangle, this side of the bungalow was much more open. It was a perfect fit for the twenty-five-plus energetic eight-to-eleven-year-old girls who made it their home each day. Off to the sides were computers and staff desks. The back wall contained four large windows that allowed plenty of light into the space. Along the front wall was a collage of Black women and girls. "I am" poems, written by the younger girls, hung above the images.

I AM
I am beautiful, kind, and smart
I wonder what I am going to be

I hear the troubles of the world
I see the world coming to an end
I want the rest of my life to be good

I AM
I am beautiful and funny
I wonder if the world can see my beauty
I hear the sounds of the sky
I see flowers when I dream
I want to make this world a better place
I am a beautiful shimmershine queen

I AM
I say that I am special
I touch the insides of my feelings
I say I can do it everyday
I pretend to be a grown lady
I dream about a good future
I say hello to God

I AM
I am intelligent and caring
I hope for blessings
I want to be myself
I am an African American girl who wonders about my life

Within each of the poems, GEP girls unapologetically and poignantly explored and expressed what it meant to be a young African American girl. Carried in these words were their hopes, fears, expectations, triumphs, and losses. These "I Am" poems spoke to GEP's construction as a space of their own, as a second home. This construction was also evident in the girls' daily routines, practices, and lessons that emphasized academic excellence, economic development, leadership development, reproductive health, and racial and gender pride.

THE DAILY FLOW

Group A girls, those between eight and eleven years old, began arriving around 2 p.m. These girls, known to staff as the early arrivals, received individual attention and focused academic help. During these moments, the bungalow was quiet. By 3 p.m., however, the energy and pace shifted, and at least twenty girls moved about the space. On the group A side, it seemed as if all the girls needed homework help, at once! Homework was their first order of business. It was what the girls, parents, and staff all said they wanted and one of the primary reasons the girls attended GEP instead of the recreation program down the hill. However, the homework period was not without contestation and signaled at the micropolitics and power negotiations that occurred on both a large and small scale within the organization.

As the noise level in the room rose, Aisha, the group A coordinator, shouted, "Fists go up!" Half of the girls responded, "Mouths go shut." Aisha repeated the call and this time the whole group responded, "Mouths go shut." As silence returned to the room, Aisha reminded the girls that this was the time for homework and that she would be moving around the room to help them. She tried to manage the demands on her time by grouping together the girls who had the same homework. This was somewhat effective, as the girls did help each other—often by sharing their answers. Every day at least two girls announced that they did not have homework, or, rather, that they had completed their homework at school. If the weather permitted, Aisha encouraged the girls to go outside and work in the garden. If the garden volunteer was not there, then often the girls resisted. They wanted to get on the computers to visit the girls visited their favorite entertainers' Web sites or download and print popular rap lyrics—lyrics that attracted the attention of the other girls. The girls were redirected—often!

Group B, on the other hand, used the time between 3 and 4 p.m. to "chill out." This was their time to check in with Maya, their coordinator, and each other. During this period, some girls went to the group A side to tutor the younger girls, others surfed the Net, and still others checked in and chatted. Their daily schedule consisted of check-in, snack, group, and then homework. Most girls arrived by 4 p.m. and in time for snack. Once snack was completed, the girls moved into "group" and the thematic lesson for the day.

Group was the heart of GEP curriculum. At GEP, group simultaneously referred to the form, content, and teaching process found within the organization. It was the space in the program where girls participated in experiential exercises, media literacy activities, or discussions that focused on what was important in the young women's lives, especially factors that impinged upon their life choices. Group curriculum was organized by the days of the week. For example, Monday was reproductive health (formerly pregnancy prevention), Tuesday was leadership development (formerly violence prevention), Wednesday was academic enrichment, Thursday was economic development, and Friday was gender and ethnic pride. Of course, these days shifted and changed depending on program needs and staff changes, but this was the basic structure. There were also special events that influenced the curriculum flow: the Black herstory celebration, the community Kwanzaa celebration, and anniversary events. These events served as vehicles for organizing curriculum units and demonstrating the girls' acquisition of new skills and knowledge. Within this loose structure, GEP staff organized and created the daily lesson plans.

For example, at GEP's five-year anniversary celebration, held in October 1998, the showcase event was "The Front Porch Dialogue: Conversations across the Generations." This conversation, a combination of performance art and loosely scripted discussions, brought together selected Black girls and women ranging from ages eleven to seventy to share Black females' multigenerational stories across several issues: teen pregnancy, poverty, HIV and AIDS, domestic violence, and gender and racial oppression.

Eleven-year-old Shayla opened the dialogue with the following poem:

> Girls are different than boys
> They have different clothes and different toys
> Girls have to worry about breast cancer, getting pregnant,
>   and puberty
> Young girls having babies worries me
> If a boy hits on a woman he is not a man
> I don't have to depend on a man because I can do for myself . . .

Before she was able to finish, the audience stood to acknowledge and celebrate her declaration of independence, female strength, and awareness of female "troubles." In fact, Shayla ended her performance on this note, leaving her poem unfinished and me with several questions regarding the process by which Shayla both created her poem and prepared for the event.

To produce the text for this performance, Shayla participated in group. As part of the five-year celebration activities, GEP sponsored an essay contest. To help the girls compose their essays, the staff gave the following writing prompts: What do you like about being a girl? What are some of the problems facing girls? In response to these questions, Shayla wrote a letter to Rosa Parks:

> Dear Ms. Rosa Parks,
> My name is Shayla . . . and I am eleven years old. I admire you because you made it possible for us to sit down in front of the bus.
> I like being a girl because you can go to clubs and programs. Girls can go to programs to help them learn about pregnancy, having children, and having a good life. If I could change some

things, I would stop men from hitting women and having sex with
women and then leaving them. I would stop men from calling
women out of their names. Women get upset when these things
happen to them and they feel sad.

> I am writing to you, Rosa Parks, because you are special to me.
> . . . You are a special woman, a hero, and a role model.

Once a draft of the essay was completed, the staff worked closely with Shayla
and the other girls to help them refine and organize their ideas. During this
revision process, the girls and the staff came together to discuss issues raised
by the young women in their essays. These issues included but were not limited to teen pregnancy, domestic violence, and discrimination. In other
words, the girls participated in group.

Group was the space within the program where GEP women and girls
discussed sex, sexuality, violence, power, and inequality, as well as Blackness,
femininity, and girlhood. It was a space that I returned to often throughout
this project to understand how Black women and girls go about the "business
of fashioning themselves" and what factors influenced such processes.

REFLECTING ON ETHNOGRAPHIC RESEARCH

I conducted the field research for this project in the San Francisco Bay Area
from August 1998 to May 2000. My initial contact with the organization
occurred in 1992. At that time I was approached by the two planning directors and invited to join a committee to create an after-school program for
girls living in low-income housing. This committee eventually became GEP's
Executive Management Committee, which created and opened GEP. I
became a member of the board of directors for the organization. As a
member of the board, I hired and fired two executive directors, and saw GEP
through its very rough first year before heading off to begin my graduate studies at Yale University. While at Yale, I kept in touch with the planning director and made periodic visits to the site. This connection not only influenced
my intellectual and research interests but also my entry into the site.

As a graduate student, I knew I wanted to think through my experiences
at GEP. The turn of events that occurred at the organization did not neatly
correspond to the literature on safe spaces and women's and girls' empowerment. At GEP, instead of alliances along race and gender lines, I witnessed
women and girls struggling with and against each other to construct and perform respectable and respected Black femininities. Additionally, these conflicts did not seem to be the result of "crazy personalities," poor management,
or incorrigible girls. Rather, I suspected that systemic forces were the cause of

staff dissatisfaction, survey reports of girls' anger, and the staff's and girls' conflicts regarding power and decision making.

When I conceived of my project and GEP looked like a match, I consulted with members of my dissertation committee as well as the GEP community about my research project. During the prospectus phase of my dissertation, I contacted GEP's executive director and we discussed my project. I told her that I was interested in how women who work with girls and the girls themselves imagine Black womanhood, and that I was particularly interested in GEP because of its Africentric womanist philosophical foundation. At that time, I offered to conduct an evaluation of the organization as an exchange of sorts for access to the site.

During the summer of 1998, my whole family, that is, my husband, my infant daughter, and I, made the cross-country journey back to the Bay Area. Unfortunately, we were not adequately prepared for changes in the Bay Area rental or job market. So when I went to discuss my research and was offered a job with the program, I did not refuse. During my job interview, with both staff and girls, my academic life was discussed in detail. They asked me about my research topic, how much time my research would take, whether it would interfere with my job performance, and how they could support me so that my studies would not suffer. I tried to explain, as someone who had just completed her proposal could, what I was interested in as a researcher, what I needed to complete my dissertation, and my time line. In fact, the executive director told me, "It is important to this organization, to all of us as Black women, that you finish, that you succeed in your work. To ensure that I am doing my part, during our supervision meetings I will be asking you about your school work." In addition, during my first year of employment at GEP, I attended a weekly seminar at U.C. Berkeley. Among staff and girls, my status as a student was out, yet my status as a researcher was often cloudy.

At first I thought that working at my primary research site was the ideal situation. In my mind I was getting paid to do my research. However, I quickly learned that my research would soon take a back seat to my work requirements. The position was incredibly demanding. As the director of programs, my job was to coordinate the delivery of services so that the organization remained true to its vision as well as complied with its grants and contracts. I supervised the four to eight direct service staff, as well as various consultants and volunteers who provided direct services to the girls. I soon found that keeping up with field notes for forty-plus hours in the field was overwhelming. To make the process of capturing my observations more manageable, I resorted to daily journal entries that documented what I saw, what I heard, what I thought, and how I felt.

As an employee, I was also concerned about the power imbalances at play within the organization. Feminist scholars note that identity plays an important role in the relationship between the researcher and her research participants (Harding 1987; Smith 1987; Collins 1991; Reinharz 1992). However, while I am an African American woman examining the experiences of predominately African American women and girls, I could not depend upon some "essentialized Blackness or womanness" as automatic passes into the world of GEP. I had to take into account the class, generational, and cultural differences that came into play. To not have done so would have been a serious methodological and sociological mistake.

I occupied varied identities and positions within GEP. Within this community of women and girls, I was a Midwestern mother and wife and perceived as privileged, and specifically middle class, based upon my educational achievement and position within the organization. Within the organizational hierarchy, I was being supervised and I was a supervisor. I was also an adult and a former member of the board of directors—considered a "founder," no less. These relationships were fraught with tension, such that layering the researcher-subject power dynamic on top felt incredibly uncomfortable.

During the year and a half that I worked at GEP, I conducted three interviews for a seminar paper. After each of these interviews there was a strange "morning-after effect." I am referring to the awkwardness that can sometimes occur after we have been intimate or shared something important with another person. For me this was intensified for two reasons: First, I was asking the staff to blur the already fragile boundaries that were in place around work or professional relationships by sharing with me their girlhoods, values, and beliefs. Second, the one-sidedness of the conversations made the disclosures feel very imbalanced. At the end of my first staff interview, Maya remarked, "Wow, by the time this is over, you'll know a lot about all of us, but we still don't know a lot about you." What was very interesting was that even when I tried to shift the interview into more of a conversation or dialogue, it was often resisted by the interviewees. For example, when I interjected my history or opinions, Maya would take back the space by looking at her watch or the clock, interrupting me, or in general acting bored. As soon as I asked another question that brought the attention back to her, the energy and interest returned. As a result of my concerns around power and my discomfort, the rest of the formal interviews were to wait until after I left my position with the organization in January 2000.

While I worked for GEP, I gathered organizational documents, took part in the day-to-day workings of the organization, and recorded what I called "hot spots" within the organizational milieu. "Hot spots," are incidents, conversations, and/or long, drawn-out conflicts that I witnessed and experienced in the organization, and they were critical to the development of this project. These hot spots were recorded in my field notes and included direct observations, recalled conversations, and my immediate analysis or questions concerning the event. During this period, I shared my fieldwork notes and emerging analyses with my writing group and faculty advisors. These conversations were critical in helping me maintain awareness of my biases, and my multiple positions within the organization. They kept in check both my romanticism and disillusionment. I also shared what I was learning and thinking with GEP staff members and girls. I often engaged the staff and girls in direct conversations about my course work and different theoretical approaches that I was "trying on" regarding women's and girls' resistance and empowerment. These were often lively conversations, during which time many of my "school" ideas were rejected, challenged, and considered. These conversations were equally important and created an ongoing opportunity for GEP members to engage and challenge me as a student, community member, and researcher. My shifting position within the organization provided me with multiple lenses through which to view the organization as well as be viewed by girls and GEP staff.

In addition, from 1999 to 2000, GEP underwent an extensive organizational evaluation, the goal of which was to develop a "replicable and powerful model" (GEP 1998). This capacity-building effort enabled staff and board members to think through the possibility of opening new sites, but most importantly it provided the resources necessary to evaluate and solidify the present work and services being delivered. It was an opportunity for the board, staff, and girls to talk "out loud" about the organization: its shortcomings and successes as well as personal hopes and dreams for the organization. The effort encouraged women and girls to make visible the invisible and to give voice to those silent spaces. It was also an opportunity for the residents and service providers of Sun Valley to think about GEP and the work carried out within and by the organization. I worked closely with the evaluators and, with clear permission from the researchers and GEP's executive director, inserted questions into the process that I thought would not only be helpful and relevant to the evaluation process but also useful to my dissertation research. As part of this process, GEP girls, staff, board members, parents, and past participants were interviewed, completed questionnaires, and participated in focus groups. Useful information from this process has been incorporated into this text and duly cited.

After I terminated my position with GEP, I conducted formal interviews with GEP women and girls. I want to make clear that although my "official" power had come to an end, my continued relationship with the organization led staff members and the girls to continue viewing me as influential. During these interviews, both staff and girls would vent and "blow the whistle" on particular staff and organizational practices they found troubling. Between January and September 2000, I interviewed thirteen or all of GEP staff members. The interviews were semi-structured and lasted between one and a half and three hours. Ten of the thirteen women identified as African American, three as of mixed racial descent. Five staff reported coming from a lower-middle to middle-middle class positions and eight from poor to working-class positions. The staff's educational background ranged from GEDs to MAs, with most having some college (including community college) but not a completed degree. While the staff ranged from ages eighteen to fifty-five, the program coordinators, who worked directly with the girls, were all young; most were in their early-to-late twenties. For many, youth work was their first work experience, and for some GEP was only their first or second salaried, as opposed to hourly, position.

I also conducted seventeen, semi-structured, tape recorded interviews with GEP girls that lasted between a half hour and two hours. While parental consent forms were distributed to all 35 GEP girls enrolled in the summer program, only seventeen were returned. These girls ranged from ages eight to seventeen, with nine girls between eight and eleven, five between twelve and fifteen, and three sixteen and above. These young women represented 65 percent of the core program participants, those girls who attend the program three to five days a week. Of the seventeen girls interviewed, thirteen self-identified as African American and four as mixed racial descent. All of the girls were residents of Sun Valley and/or had family that lived in the public housing development. Given public housing restrictions, it is not surprising that most, fifteen out of seventeen, reported living in a female-headed household, though not always with their biological mothers. Additionally, sixteen out of seventeen reported being eligible for free or reduced-fee lunch. On average, the girls had attended the program between two and five years.

The interview protocol developed for this study asked girls and staff to share their experiences with GEP, what they liked about the organization, what they disliked, what changes they would make, and their sense of power within and outside of GEP. To begin the interview, girls and staff completed a brief demographic questionnaire. The interviews provided the girls and staff an opportunity to tell me in their own words and in response to direct questions what they thought and why it mattered.

Once transcribed, I read and reread the interview transcripts, supporting documents, and my ongoing field notes to see what patterns and themes emerged from the data. Using the work of Frankenberg (1993) and Luttrell (1997) as working models, I began to analyze the narratives in terms of internal coherence, in relation to each other, and in context of a broader social history (Frankenberg 1993, 42). In my reading and analysis, I focused on places where girls and staff addressed their ideas and feelings about voice, choice, and power within the organization and beyond. Once identified, I reread the transcripts and documents, highlighting and coding for these themes.

At this time I also conducted formal observations. During my visits, I would hang out in the bungalow with the staff and the girls. I also attended special events hosted by the organization. For example, I attended several Black herstory celebrations and Kwanzaa events. While observing, I was particularly interested in the ways that staff and girls talked about power, empowerment, and Black womanhood. I was also interested in the constructions of femininity that GEP participants, staff, board members, and parents were using. Such cultural scripts tell us about what is acceptable and unacceptable. While it was always clear that portions of the cultural scripts of Black femininity shared elements with White middle-class, or what Collins (2004) would call "hegemonic" femininity, I was curious where these converged and differed.

Finally, between March 2000 and August 2000, I visited four girl-serving organizations in the Bay Area: a private Catholic all-girls high school, a girls-only program in a neighboring public housing development, a Girls Inc. program, and a program for young women in the street economy. In addition, I participated in a videotaped roundtable discussion with six girl-serving organizations in the Bay Area. The purpose of visiting these programs and participating in these discussions was twofold: one, to see if what I was observing at my primary site was the result of some idiosyncratic processes, or if they were common to other girl-serving organizations and to what extent; and, two, because the visits allowed me to locate GEP within the world of girl-serving organizations and the girls' movement.

When I began this project, I had dreams of creating a critical ethnography detailing the complicated relationships and negotiations over representations of Black femininity between well-meaning Black women and the amazingly insightful and resilient Black girls they served. However, while retaining ethnographic methods, I modified my methodology to a qualitative case study. The shift did several things. First and foremost, while it did not remove concerns of representation, voice, and power, it correctly shifted the "subject" of study. Within a qualitative case study, one is interested in "a specific, unique, bounded system," and the qualitative data, of which participant observation is only a part, serves to illustrate the case (Stake 1995, 274). As a result of careful consideration of the data gathered from the field, a qualitative case study seemed a better fit for the sociological questions I was pursuing and the better form for presenting the material. Thus I focused more on the events and exchanges within the organization to elucidate the configuration of power and constructions of femininity within GEP. This is not to say that this case does not focus on the women's and girls' lives; it does. However, I do not purport to tell a story about Black women's and girls' lives at large; I only attempt to speak to their relationships within this organization and what that can tell us about women's and girls' construction and maintenance of safe spaces, their resistance to negative representations, and the impact of the organization on both of these processes.

As noted earlier, this shift does not eliminate questions of power and representation. I struggled with the tension between my shifting insider/outsider status and positions of power. Specifically, the more details I attempted to reveal about GEP women's and girls' lives, the more anxiety I experienced. That is, knowing how representations of Black women and girls are distorted and used to maintain social and power imbalances in this country, I began to feel uncomfortable displaying and publicly presenting the struggles of the girls and women to whom I had grown particularly close. I was also struggling with my own voice and experience. How was I going represent myself? How much of my life was going to be revealed? And how much voice would I give myself as the inside-out participant versus the outside-in observer? The more I contemplated these issues of representation and power, the more anxiety I felt. At times it was paralyzing. At other times I knew that challenging dominant discourses could shift the terrain. And if I could provide a mirror for myself and other women and girls in the girls' movement, then I knew I had an obligation to put pen to paper and write/represent the women and girls who courageously shared their voices with me, with the expectation that I would tell my story.

In the end, this is my informed sociological analysis of what I experienced, saw, heard, and felt during my time at GEP. As such, it is caught up in who I am. In many ways the research process and the text represent my own intellectual, educational, and political journey and tell the story of how my understanding has shifted during my ten-plus-year relationship with GEP. That said, I also believe it speaks to larger theoretical questions concerning identity, culture, and power.

2

Controlling "The Urban Girl"

Even on the bus, like when I was on the bus and I'll go somewhere, if a guy approaches me and ask me where I'm from and I be like, "I'm not from anywhere," and he be like, "Well, I mean, where you from?" . . . and it is automatically, "Ah," and they wait a couple minutes. "Do you got any kids?" "No, I don't have kids. Try askin' me if I can read, fool." You know? I mean, and it's—I mean, there's just this automatic—like they automatically suspect or assume that you have to have a house full of kids or that you have to be on welfare. "I don't have any kids!" I can't be a young woman who's moved out just by gaining independence. I'm on my way to college. I can't be that? I have to be this person who's sort of stuck. (Nyema, GEP girl and intern, age seventeen)

Black girls, especially working-class and low-income girls living in our cities, must learn to navigate the stereotype of "The Urban Girl." "The Urban Girl" is the young Black female face that haunts the workfare and welfare debates and floats through academic and social discourses on sexuality, female-headed households, and urban poverty (Tolman 1996). Rooted within the historical representation of Black women as breeder women, this stereotype rose to prominence during the 1980s and served as the "human face" of the nation's social anxieties about shifting economic, sexual, and social trends understood through the lens of teen pregnancy (Davis 1981; Collins 1991; Luker 1996; Roberts 1997).

According to Tolman (1996), "The Urban Girl"

> is not a real person but a unidimensional stick figure who lives in the public imagination rather than on the streets of urban America. On the body of The Urban Girl, social context becomes confused and confounded with race: she is a girl of color, and so she must be poor [Painter 1992]. She is the daughter of a single mother. She is incapable of delaying gratification, fails in school, does not secure employment, and most of all she is sexually promiscuous, lacking in morality or family values, and out of control. She is at risk and at fault. (1996, 255–56)

Stereotypes are socially constructed representations that intersect with systems of oppression and "function as a disguise, or mystification, of objective social relations" (Carby 1987, 22). In other words, as components of ideological systems, they justify and legitimate oppression by making unequal treatment seem like the "natural" consequence of innate or essential characteristics of the subordinate group (Carby 1987; Collins 1991). "The Urban Girl," intertwined with her sister stereotypes "teen mom," "unwed mother," and "welfare queen," "transmits clear messages about the proper links between female sexuality, fertility, and Black women's roles in the political economy" (Collins 1991, 78).

GEP's organizational environment was defined by the "teen pregnancy epidemic" of the 1980s and early 1990s and represented by the figure of "The Urban Girl." As noted earlier, an organization's environment is characterized by the key material and ideological milieus that impact its creation, survival, and success (DiMaggio and Powell 1991[1983]; Fried 1994; Bordt 1997). Scholars have found that resource dependencies can influence the mission, goals, structures, and success of organizations, particularly neighborhood nonprofits (DiMaggio and Powell 1991[1983]; Milofsky and Romo 1988; Gamson 1996).

In this chapter, I examine GEP's organizational environment. I suggest that during the moment of GEP's emergence, the nation's collective anxieties regarding the shifting sexual trends and economic dislocations were thought to be caused by teen pregnancy and blamed on "The Urban Girl." As a result, both dominant and indigenous group members sought to control the sexuality, reproduction, and "dependency" of poor Black girls. Moreover, GEP's institutional context—that area defined by GEP's identity as a nonprofit service organization linked to other organizations through resource opportunities and dependencies—supported this discourse of control. That is, in a period of shrinking economic opportunities and increased competition within the nonprofit sector, both governmental and philanthropic organizations concentrated funds to reduce welfare dependency and its purported cause teen pregnancy, thereby encouraging and supporting the growth and development of programs such as GEP.

TEEN PREGNANCY AND THE SPECTER OF "THE URBAN GIRL"

In her book *Dubious Conceptions*, Kristin Luker (1996) found that during the 1980s, academics, politicians, and the public lined up to make sense of the expansion of poverty and what seemed to be a rise in out-of-wedlock teenage pregnancies. She suggests the following:

> As the dire statistics made their way from research journals to Congress to the media and then acquired the status of conventional wisdom, the association between early childbearing and poverty (asserting that where we find one, we find the other) moved from a correlation to a causative relationship. Since teenage parents were more often poorer, less educated, and more liable to problematic pregnancies than older women, the public soon found it logical to assume that early childbearing caused these conditions. (110–11)

Thus despite data suggesting that teen pregnancies were on the decline, that most single mothers were not teens, and that poor women were very likely to remain poor whether or not they had children as teens, an epidemic was constructed that identified teen mothers, in particular Black teenage mothers, as a way to address Americans' collective anxieties regarding changes in women's sexual, reproductive, and labor market activity, as well as the overall decline in the nation's economy. Teenage pregnancy became a social issue that contained and explained the expansion of poverty and, more important, the expansion of welfare dependency in the United States (Luker 1996).

However, while this "rise" in teen pregnancy, and the social and sexual trends it represented therein, was a cause for concern, it was not enough to create the "epidemic" of the 1980s. Rather, in the midst of this great social transformation in women's reproductive choice and labor market participation, Americans were also experiencing economic anxieties not felt since the Great Depression. It was the coupling of these social and sexual trends with the economic displacement that moved teen pregnancy from a trend to an "epidemic" (Luker 1996).

During the late 1960s, the U.S. economy underwent a major shift from a manufacturing to a service economy that profoundly altered the urban labor market. During this period, capitalists in search of greater profits moved their factories from central cities to rural non-unionized areas or outside of the United States to employ cheaper labor. The result was a deindustrialization of the central cities and massive economic dislocation.[1] This new economy, driven by growth in technology, financial/producer services, and the health care sectors, shut low-skilled, poorly educated workers out of higher-wage occupations by demanding high levels of specialized education and locked them into low-wage, generally non-union, dead-end service jobs—thus creating new inequalities in our urban cores (Wilson 1987; Sassen 1994). In other words, "while the manufacturing-based economies that boomed during the 1960s contributed to the expansion of a middle class and deterred systemic tendencies toward inequality by constituting an economic regime centered on mass production and mass consumption," city dwellers in the service economy experienced a two-tiered labor market that fostered a sharp polarization between the professional service providers and those that serve the professionals (Sassen 1994, 101).[2] Beginning with the economic shifts of the late 1960s and continuing into the 1990s, the quality of life for Blacks living in the urban cores deteriorated dramatically. The economic displacement, coupled with the government-sponsored suburbanization effort, facilitated a massive migration of Whites out of the central cities into the suburbs, creating what George Clinton, member of the funk band Parliament, described as "chocolate cities and vanilla suburbs." As noted in chapter 1, these macro-structural social and economic shifts were reflected in Sun Valley, the home of GEP and the girls they served.

Amid these social and economic dislocations, conservative political demands for a change in government priorities were growing. In response to these demands—starting in the 1970s, accelerated by the Reagan administration, and continued by the George H. Bush and Clinton administrations—the federal government began the process of dismantling the welfare state. In 1981, Reagan announced the following:

> With the same energy that Franklin Roosevelt sought government solutions to problems, we will seek private solutions. The challenge before us is to find ways once again to unleash the independent spirit of people and their communities. (as quoted in Salamon 1995, 149)

True to its word, after almost five decades of government expansion in the provision of human services, the Reagan administration, with its Omnibus Budget and Reconciliation Act of 1981 and its Economic Recovery Tax Act of the same year, drastically cut funding for domestic programs. At a time when Americans, especially African American residents of the central cities, needed a government-sponsored safety net the most, Reaganomics, or the Reagan administration's "trickle down" economic recovery plan, provided little relief. Key to the dismantling of the welfare state was the reevaluation of the welfare program and a vitriolic attack on welfare recipients, especially poor Black women deemed undeserving.[3]

Reagan, in 1980, "promised that he would rid the welfare system of cheaters and those who could work but were receiving welfare" (as quoted in Sheared 1998, 36). In his 1986 State of the Union Address, he blamed welfare for the "breakdown of the family," and he said the "welfare culture" was responsible for "female and child poverty, child abandonment, horrible crimes, and deteriorating schools" (as quoted in Amott 1990, 290). As part of his program, he urged young girls to " 'just say no,' so taxpayers would not have to pay for their sexual behavior," and publicly solidified the causal link between teen pregnancy, the expansion of poverty, and welfare dependency (as quoted in Kaplan 1997, xx). Thus underlying the federal government's cuts in spending were ideological assumptions about teen pregnancy and welfare. Of particular note was Reagan's infamous "welfare queen."

Reagan vowed not just to rid the system of generic welfare cheaters—he focused specifically on "welfare queens." These so called "queens of the ghetto," dubbed so because they lived like "royalty" at taxpayers' expense, were the "ultimate 'rational actors' of neoclassical economics: they assessed the costs of having a baby, analyzed the benefits of welfare, and 'invested' in a course of action that would get them what they want" (Luker 1996, 4). In other words, they had more children to increase the amount of their welfare checks and to keep from working. The problem, however, was not their logic, it was that this logic was not put to use in the appropriate "labor market." Lubiano (1992) writes:

> "Welfare queen" is a phrase that describes economic dependency—the lack of a job and/or income (which equal degeneracy in the Calvinist United States); the presence of a child or children with no father and/or husband (moral deviance); and, finally, a charge on the collective U.S. treasury—a human debit. . . . The welfare queen represents moral aberration and an economic drain, but the figure's problematic status becomes all the more threatening once responsibility for the destruction of the "American way of life" is attributed to it. (337–38)

The welfare queen became synonymous with the poor Black mother living in our nation's ghettos—unwed, unemployed, undesired, and undeserving.[4] Charged with creating and literally reproducing a culture of poverty, she and her children robbed the country of its moral and economic resources.

By refusing to participate in the labor market, Black welfare mothers challenged the racialized gender codes that constructed Black women as breeders and workers, not mothers (Davis 1981; Collins 1991). In so doing, as capable workers they challenged the Protestant ethic that equates morality with productivity. As such, "The Urban Girl," constructed as both immanent and imminent unwed mothers and welfare queens, came to represent the nation's "human debit."

The Reagan administration also constructed Aid to Families with Dependent Children (AFDC) as a program that "enabled women to live without a husband or job" and thus placed the "welfare queen" and, by proxy, "The Urban Girl," as women outside the control of husbands, fathers, and/or patriarchal state institutions (as quoted in Amott 1990, 290).[5] As a result, both Black women and girls must be forced to stop having sex, forced to marry, forced to work, forced to limit their reproductive capacity, and forced to allow others to "properly care for" and resocialize their children. In other words, they must be forced to submit to the "American way of life"—that particular sexist and racist version reserved for poor Black women.

Teen mothers were subjected to increasing levels of surveillance and control. The New Right took the lead in this project and sought to reestablish parental control of girls' sexuality, reproduction, and welfare dependency. According to Luker (1996):

> Conservatives sought not merely to cope with the social trends that had taken place in the past decades, but actually to reverse them. With respect to early pregnancy and childbearing, for example, the problem was not teenagers' pregnancies but their sexual activity; the remedy was not contraception but chastity; and thus attention should be devoted not to the young women but to her family, who needed help in regaining its control over her. (76)

Key to the conservative agenda was the restoration of family as the primary vehicle for maintaining control over young girls' sexuality and, by extension, reproduction and welfare dependency. They used resource withdrawal, legislative activities, and direct actions to reinstate "traditional" (patriarchal) values in families, schools, and places of employment (Hyde 1995, 313–14).[6]

Moreover, if patriarchal control could not be restored via the family, the New Right's social policies supported the intrusion of state-sponsored patriarchy into the young women's lives. The federal government reduced and restricted girls' access to safe sex education and birth control distribution in schools, eliminated the Family Planning Fund, criminalized abortion, and, in some cases, advocated involuntary Norplant insertions and sterilization (Hyde 1995; Luker 1996; Roberts 1997).

For those who failed to heed the "Just Say No" edict and became pregnant, the state sought to remove the financial "incentives" for childbearing and single parenthood through benefit reductions, a more restrictive means test to determine "deserving" and "undeserving" recipients, and coupling welfare with mandatory work and educational training programs—a movement culminating in the Clinton administration's Personal Responsibility and Work Reconciliation Opportunity Act (PRWORA), passed in 1996 (Hyde 1995; Luker 1996).[7] Reflecting upon the state's control over poor women, Johnnie Tillmon, the first chairwoman of the National Welfare Rights Organization, asserted:

> The truth is that AFDC is like a supersexist marriage. You trade in a man for the man. . . . In ordinary marriage, sex is supposed to be for your husband. On AFDC, you're not supposed to have any sex at all. You give up control of your own body. It's a condition of aid. (as quoted in Amott 1990, 289)

In the end, the state sought to reinvigorate public control over "out of control" women and girls.

Yet this control over poor Black girls' bodies was not just the purview of dominant institutions and the "American public." The Black community, especially Black women in the community, also sought to control the sexuality, reproduction, and economic dependency of poor Black girls. That is, while often constructed as supporters of teen pregnancy, most members of various Black communities viewed teen mothers as deviant. Luker (1996) found:

> Even the group thought to be most accepting of unwed teenage mothers—the African American community—is far more disapproving than most people think. Acceptance of a teenage mother or father is not the same as approval: young mothers, both Black and white, often report widespread censure from those around them. Their own mothers, many of who were once teenage mothers themselves and were hoping for a better life for their daughters, sometimes express disappointment bordering on rage. (135)

Across class lines, for many African Americans, teenage motherhood was not acceptable. In Kaplan's (1997) ethnography of Black teenage mothers, her respondents detailed the myriad ways they were shamed, shunned, and ostracized by members of the African American community. Neighbors, peers, church members, and teachers all said "terrible things about them" (Kaplan 1997, 153). In fact, despite widespread belief that Black mothers condoned and supported their daughters' sexual activity and reproductive choices, they were perhaps the most disapproving. Many advocated abortions, often growing angry when their daughters refused. Kaplan argues that for them "teenage pregnancy breaks several important long-standing cultural norms greatly valued by adult Black mothers"—most important, economic security and class status (1997, 69).[8] At rock bottom, their daughters had failed them.

Similarly, in her ethnographic work, Fordham (1996) found that Black girls, especially high-achieving Black girls, experienced "pervasive parental control." She notes:

> A common, relentless goal in the childrearing practices . . . is control of their daughters' lives and even of the options they consider. The central lesson the mothers taught was the value of behaving in socially appropriate ways (conformity)—most important, not bringing shame on the family by acting on their developing sexuality. (146)

Black girls' whereabouts were heavily monitored and controlled. They were required to attend church and subjected to strict curfews and dating restrictions that explicitly and unconsciously articulated their parents' "fear" of their daughters' "developing sexuality" (Fordham 1996, 121). Thus members of the Black community, and in particular Black mothers, were not immune to discourse that made a causal connection between teen pregnancy and poverty. Once this connection was made, Black community members, similar to politicians, academics, and media representatives, shifted from addressing the structural sources of poverty to controlling Black girls' sexuality (Collins 1991). It was within this social-political context that GEP emerged and developed.

GEP'S RESOURCE DEPENDENCIES
AND INSTITUTIONAL CONTEXT

GEP began as a sponsored project of Bay City's Women's Building. As a sponsored project, the Women's Building served as GEP's fiscal agent and provided umbrella nonprofit status. That is, the Women's Building, for a fee, accepted tax-deductible grants and gifts on behalf of GEP, as well as assumed legal and fiscal responsibility, thereby encouraging potential funders to take a protected risk on an emerging program. The relationship gave GEP legitimacy. As a result, the fledgling organization was able to tap into the realm of public and private dollars—dollars it would not have been able to generate from its clientele or the larger Bay City Black community. At the time of its emergence, however, GEP had to negotiate changes in its institutional sector—informed by the teen pregnancy epidemic and driven by the disappearing welfare state—that dramatically impacted its search for funding and ultimately supported its organizational goals, emergence, survival, and success.

Prior to the mid-1960s, funding from private donations, religious organizations, and the United Way supported most nonprofit organizations (O'Neil 1989). With the great society programs of the 1960s, massive amounts of federal, state, and local government money were funneled into nonprofit organizations through various grants and contracts (O'Neil 1989; Wolch 1990; Salamon 1995). However, with the election of Ronald Reagan, the shape of the nonprofit service sector changed. In a contradictory move, Reagan simultaneously cut federal government funding for social services, many of which were being carried out by nonprofit service organizations, while calling for an increased reliance upon this sector for the provision of such services (Harder et al. 1985; Musselwhite et al. 1987; Salamon 1995). The results were dramatic.

In Bay City, for example, government spending on human services declined by a cumulative total of $134 million in 1982, 1983, and 1984, compared to the amounts that would have been available had 1981 spending levels been maintained (Musselwhite et al. 1987). Simultaneously, there was an increase in the number of nonprofit public benefit organizations serving the poor and single-parent families. Myllyluoma and Salamon (1992) found that between 1982 and 1990, the proportion of Bay City agencies primarily serving the poor increased from 24 percent to 32 percent, and those serving single-parent families increased from 11 percent to 16 percent (16). Even more striking is that the proportion of organizations with no poor clients fell from 34 percent to 23 percent, and those with no single-parent families declined from 49 percent to 22 percent (Myllyluoma and Salamon 1992, 16). Despite this increase in service, federal government funding accounted for a smaller share of nonprofits' total revenues as compared to pre-1982 dollars (Myllyluoma and Salamon 1992). Thus as a direct result of the disappearing welfare state, organizations reported turning to alternative sources of funding and in the process faced increased competition for limited funds.

At the time of GEP's emergence, the highly publicized Rodney King beating and subsequent uprising in Los Angeles over the acquittal of the assaulting police officers made visible the disappearing welfare state and unmet needs within our cities.[9] Immediately following the rebellion in South Central, both private foundations and government agencies began rethinking conditions in urban cores. As a result, money was made available to address the social and economic issues facing residents in South Central and similar communities within California and the United States at large. While the focus of many of the new grants was on youth services, job creation, and development, given the gendered rhetoric of the culture of poverty, reducing welfare dependency and teen pregnancy simmered just beneath the surface. Foundations targeted these areas for funding and investigation, and government at all levels instituted programs to reduce teen pregnancy and the social outcomes thought to result from early motherhood (Luker 1996, 81). Welfare dependency, and its purported cause, teen pregnancy, among low-income Black girls living in urban cities, was an issue ripe for public support, funding, and media publicity—important factors in an organization's creation, survival, and success. In other words, while many nonprofits suffered as a result of federal cuts, funding for economic self-sufficiency and teen pregnancy reduction was strong.

In the midst of this national concern regarding welfare dependency and teen pregnancy, GEP entered into an under resourced and competitive institutional context and developed a three prong approach to funding. First, the organization looked toward independent, community, and corporate foundations to provide start-up funding for the first three years.[10] Second, public support via city, state, and federal monies was targeted as both start-up and long-term funding opportunities. Finally, GEP board worked to create an individual donor base for long-term funding and sustainability. This three-prong strategy was developed by Melinda George.

As noted earlier, Melinda secured a $50,000 planning grant from the San Francisco Foundation to research what services were available for girls. This grant, in part driven by the AAUW Report on "Shortchanging Girls" and the resulting media, was also tied to Melinda, who had extensive experience and success in creating and managing organizations for and by women. In addition, she had over twenty years of experience writing grants and developing relationships with local grant makers. Funders, wary of providing financial support to a new organization, may have been more inclined to take a risk because of their relationship with Melinda, as well as her reputation and track record. One grant-making organization representative noted, "We had worked with Melinda before and we knew the project was in good hands if she was involved."[11] In other words, while funding commitments for economic self-sufficiency (read welfare reduction) and teen pregnancy reduction were increasing within the grant-making world, Melinda's reputation and organization-building skills facilitated the funding of GEP.[12]

At the center of GEP's fund-raising strategy was the solicitation of grants from foundations. In fact, foundation requests made up 76 percent of GEP's proposed start-up budget (GEP 1992b). Specifically, GEP targeted seven private family, three community, and six corporate foundations.[13] These foundations ranged in size. For example, in 1992, GEP was awarded a $10,000 grant from the Friedman Family Foundation, a small private family foundation that granted a total of approximately $150,000 to local nonprofits working with low-income youth and families that year (Friedman Family Foundation 1992). Simultaneously, GEP successfully secured a $165,000 three-year start-up grant from the San Francisco Foundation, a community foundation that during the 1991–1992 fiscal year granted almost $20 million to local nonprofits (San Francisco Foundation 1992).[14]

As noted earlier, many foundations were concerned with worsening conditions in U.S. urban centers. For example, the James Irvine Foundation, another early financial backer of GEP, spoke of a "deep soul searching over its past decisions, possible responses and future actions" in the wake of the riots and rebellion following the acquittal of the LAPD officers. In its 1992 *Annual Report*, the foundation noted that

> the events of 1992 encouraged the Foundation to face up to race . . . and confirmed that issues such as poverty, unemployment, education, family life, and violence are affected by public policies and the ability to advocate for just solutions, equitable access and appropriate resources. (James Irvine Foundation 1992)

Addressing the short- and long-term needs of the residents and institutions within central cities became a funding priority among many foundations.

For funders, GEP was a shining example of how the conditions in urban areas could be addressed. The program appeared to tackle both outcomes and causes, with its focus on young women and tenants. For example, GEP was highlighted as a new member of the Irvine Foundation's funding family in its *Annual Report*. The program served as an exemplary model of the foundation's goal to

> improve the economic and social well-being of the disadvantaged and their communities, foster self-sufficiency, and assist ethnic minorities to function more effectively as full participants in society. (James Irvine Foundation 1992)

During its start-up phase GEP also approached the Stuart Foundation, which was "interested in efforts that promote economic stability in neighborhoods and provide enhanced opportunities for a stable base of educated and skilled working residents,"[15] as well as the Friedman Family Foundation, which worked to "introduce new programs and policies that allow those on the margins of the economy a reasonable chance to craft their own futures."[16]

While reducing teen pregnancy was not explicitly identified within any of the foundations' stated objectives, phrases such as "self-sufficiency," "craft their own futures," and "function more effectively" served as code words that addressed the race, class, and gender issues at hand. Unspoken yet lurking within these objectives was the culture of poverty discourse that saw poor Black teenage mothers and welfare dependency as the cause of such issues. In other words, available funds encouraged organizations such as GEP to change the girls as opposed to changing the social policies and structures that created many of the problems. GEP tapped into this rhetoric and created a program for "tomorrow's mothers."

As part of the competitive hunt for private and public dollars, GEP had to construct a request for funding proposal (RFP), its public face to the funding world. RFPs serve as structured and ritualized forms of communication between the organizations requesting funding and grant-making agencies. They serve to explicitly connect the grant-seeking organization's project with that of the grant-making organization's mission and to describe the objectives or outcomes to be achieved through a specific and measurable lens. Successful applicants understand and know what a grant-making organization is looking for, who has been successfully funded, and the latest fad sweeping across the funding community. They also know what specific outcomes count as fundable and measurable.

In its first request for funding, GEP wrote:

> Many of today's inner-city 11-year-old girls are on the verge of becoming welfare-dependent teen mothers, who, most ominously for the future, will be passing on to their children a psychological legacy of passivity and despair, failure and poverty, violence and victimization that in all likelihood their mothers passed on to them. These girls are growing up with babies and a welfare check the only vision on their horizon, welfare dependency having become an intergenerational way of life. (GEP 1992b, 1)

GEP constructed its potential clients as "Urban Girls" or immanent mothers and welfare queens. In so doing, it explicitly connected its organizational mission and program outcomes to the resource opportunities of the moment. This is not to say that the stated goals and outcomes did not represent the founders' "authentic" beliefs but, rather, to note that with each RFP, many nonprofit organizations emphasize and highlight particular features to connect with each prospective funder. Given the circulation of the culture of poverty and teen pregnancy narratives, as well as the deteriorating conditions of the "inner city" during this period, GEP's stated goals matched the call for proposals put forth by many foundations. In the process, the organization constructed poor Black girls in a deficit manner and positioned the organization as a solution to issues of welfare dependency, violence, and teen pregnancy.[17]

Philanthropic organizations, embedded within the larger social political context, were not immune to the "teen pregnancy epidemic" rhetoric and culture of poverty discourse. Foundations funded programs that redressed poverty through assisting poor Black girls to stay in school and to become economically self-sufficient. Thus despite federal government cuts, private foundations made resources available for reducing poverty (read "reducing teen pregnancy and economic dependency among poor Black girls"). In organizational terms, there was an open niche for GEP.

To augment private foundation grants, GEP also applied for public funding. It secured a Housing Authority grant aimed at "empowering tenants and increasing their investment in their communities . . . and involvement in the development of social services in their communities" (GEP 1992b, 20). This grant was an important part of the organization's start-up and supported the job development and training of the local residents. It was, however, only a short-term funding solution, and it did not provide the funds to sustain tenant development and employment over the years. Perhaps the most important public funds GEP secured were Proposition J funds received from the Mayor's Office of Children Youth and Families (MOCYF). The monies from the city allowed the organization to "keep the door open" and to maintain a basic level of service throughout the research period. The MOCYF funds were the most stable and consistent source of funding for the GEP, and Ife considered it to be GEP's "bread and butter" because it paid for most staff salaries. These monies were a direct result of the 1991 passage of Proposition J, or the Children's Amendment, which increased the property tax to pay for children and youth services. Finally, GEP constructed a donor database that targeted African American individuals and groups. The founders envisioned an individual donor base that would "provide a basis for ongoing community support and will strengthen the connection between the socioeconomic classes" (GEP 1992b, 20). While such individual and group donations were small, they succeeded in keeping the program and African American girls visible within the local African American community.

Ylvisaker (1987) notes that grant-making power lies in "money and the power that goes with it" (372). With this power, grant-making agencies, including both public and private organizations, exert substantial influence over both the nonprofit sector and public affairs through the targeting of issues and concentration of funds (see Helfgot [1974]1981). By creating funding opportunities that emphasized economic self-sufficiency, especially

through the reduction of teen pregnancy, both public and private foundations created an institutional context that supported the sociopolitical pressure to control the sexuality, reproduction, and dependency of poor Black
girls and encouraged and shaped GEP's emergence.

In sum, GEP emerged during the "teen pregnancy epidemic" of the late
1980s and early 1990s and encountered a social-political and institutional
discourse that defined "The Urban Girl" as the face of teenage pregnancy
and poverty. Key to this discourse was the Reagan administration's dismantling of the welfare state and the strengthening of both public and private
patriarchal control over teenage girls in general and Black girls in particular.
As part of this effort, Reagan blamed "welfare queens" and, by proxy, poor
Black girls for the nation's economic troubles; made drastic cuts in federal
welfare funds and services, especially those targeting the sexual and reproductive rights of teens; and called for increased dependence on the private
nonprofit sectors. GEP's resource environment, embedded within this larger
sociopolitical context and composed primarily of private philanthropic
organizations and government-sponsored funding, supported this discourse of
control over Black girls' bodies. Through targeted funding, especially within
a competitive and resource-scarce institutional sector, these funding organizations exerted normative pressures on GEP, which it subsequently reproduced in an effort to acquire funds. This discourse, however, was not the sole
purview of conservatives. Both liberals and conservatives, Blacks and
Whites, and rich and poor alike lamented over the problem of teen pregnancy and struggled to find both a discourse and practice to explain it. For
GEP founders, an ideology grounded in notions of empowerment provided
the answers.

3

GEP's Emergent Culture of Empowerment

There ain't no GEP failures, because GEP is a pretty open and loving place.

—Diamond, GEP girl, age twelve

GEP grew out of the sociopolitical context and dominant discourses encircling the lives of poor Black girls during the late 1980s and early 1990s. To address the plight of "The Urban Girl," the founders, of which I was a part, developed an after-school program for low-income African American girls. Our initial mission statement read:

> The Girls Empowerment Project is a new primary and secondary prevention program aimed at interrupting the intergenerational cycle of teen pregnancy, welfare dependency, school drop-out, low self-esteem, and substance abuse on the part of low-income, inner city, at-risk girls who live in Bay City public housing. (GEP 1992b, 1)

Drawing upon social science and popular discourse on the culture of poverty, we constructed poor Black girls as future welfare mothers who passed on the "legacy of poverty" to their children. Our goal was to "intervene in their lives before the downward trajectory becomes irreversible, that is, beginning at age 11, before they have become pregnant and their self-esteem has been lost" (GEP 1992b, 5). The founders identified girlhood as an opportunity and pushed for the creation of a "culturally enriched educational" program for poor Black girls or "tomorrow's mothers—the most critical factor in perpetuating the intergenerational cycle of poverty" (GEP 1992b, 3). We attempted to create an organization and organizational culture that fostered girls' empowerment.

Empowerment is an often-used yet problematic concept. Empowerment has been defined as "giving girls voice" (Brown and Gilligan 1990). Within this paradigm, empowerment often implies a one-way process of power sharing from women to girls that silently maintains power differentials. Moreover, this particular use of the term also overlooks the power that those "in need of empowerment," or the girls, bring to the table. Given our limited view of empowerment and, more importantly, power at the time, we laid the groundwork for an organizational culture where consciousness-raising, voice, and safe space were supported with the intent of giving girls the necessary self-esteem to counter the debilitating circumstances of poverty.

Organizational culture—the shifting and often-competing networks of meaning within organizations—shapes and "reflects how members think things should be and how things really are" (Lord and Maher 1991). One key to analyzing an organization's culture is the mission statement. Mission statements "serve as the foundation for the assumptions, values and beliefs on which an organization's culture is based" (Zammuto, Gifford, and Goodman 2000, 264). They articulate the critical ideologies of the organization, putting into place interpretative frames with which to make sense of organizational life. Such ideologies, whether accepted or rejected by members of the organization, guide and shape the organization's structure, goals, practices, and survival strategies (Hyde 1995) as well as rationalize and legitimate patterns of authority and decision making (Beyer 1981). Examining the construction and revision of GEP's mission statement proves important for illuminating the organization's emerging culture of empowerment.

In this chapter, I examine GEP's organizational culture, paying particular attention to the creation and transformation of the organization's mission statement. I suggest that GEP's founders drew upon the class, race, and gender reforms of the period to develop a culturally relevant, single-sex, after-school program designed to empower Black girls living in public housing. Grounded in these discourses, GEP developed strategies to assist girls in overcoming structural barriers and social factors such as racism, sexism, poverty, and limited educational opportunities to achieve equal access and equal outcomes. This discourse of empowerment provided the interpretative framework necessary for members to revise the mission statement, redefine Black girls as resilient and powerful, and ultimately construct an explicitly Africentric womanist space and organizational identity.

DOMINANT DISCOURSES GIVE RISE TO SOLUTIONS

GEP's goals were to improve girls' life chances by

> instilling gender and ethnic pride through female and culturally rel-
> evant history, art and role models, increasing chances for academic
> and later vocational success, improving family and peer relation-
> ships, preventing unwanted teen pregnancy, promoting economic
> development (i.e., increase the skills they need to achieve financial
> self-sufficiency) and providing opportunities for aspirations and
> dreams. (GEP 1992b, 16–17)

In other words, we attempted to create a program where girls, especially poor
Black girls, could shore up their self-esteem and thereby achieve academic
success and economic self-sufficiency. Yet just as the representations of poor
Black girls and the problems they faced were located within the larger social
political context, so too were elements of the proposed solution. During the
period of GEP's emergence, three reform discourses circulated that addressed
poor Black girls' day-to-day realities and informed the program's design and
emerging culture of empowerment. Specifically, William J. Wilson (1987)
posited a class-based structural reform, and Afrocentrists and feminist argued,
respectively, for race-based and gender-based educational cultural reforms.
Underlying these reform efforts were ideological frameworks explaining the
cause and effect of class, race, and gender oppression facing poor Black girls.
From these efforts, GEP's founders developed an organizational culture that
promoted Black girls' empowerment.

INTERRUPTING GHETTO-SPECIFIC CULTURE

In *The Truly Disadvantaged*, Wilson (1987) outlined the significance of
poverty in the lives of those living in our cities' ghettos. He identified the
loss of jobs and the flight of the Black middle and working classes out of the
ghettos as two structural factors that helped create and sustain the "Truly
Disadvantaged."[1] According to Wilson, during the era of segregation, in periods of economic downturn, Black communities drew upon the human, social,
cultural, and economic capital of the middle and working classes and were
able to maintain "a sense of community, positive neighborhood identifica-
tion, and explicit norms against aberrant behavior" (Wilson 1987, 60).
These "working" families served as links to employment networks as well as
role models that reinforced mainstream values regarding work, educational

attainment, and family stability. As a result, they acted as a "social buffer" by maintaining the stability of social institutions within Black communities.

However, with the exodus of the Black middle and working classes from the central cities during the late 1960s and early 1970s, those left behind existed in "social isolation" with little contact and sustained interaction with individuals and institutions that represented mainstream behaviors and values. The response to these structural constraints and limited opportunities was the creation of a "ghetto-specific culture"—a social milieu characterized by "massive joblessness, flagrant and open lawlessness," welfare dependency, and family instability (Wilson 1987, 58). In other words, in contrast to theorists who describe a "culture of poverty" that is self-perpetuating and almost permanent in nature, Wilson argued that ghetto-specific culture is a historical response to economic and social conditions that could be "eventually changed" with structural, specifically economic, changes. As a result, when looking to create change, he argued:

> Programs created to alleviate poverty, joblessness, and related forms of social dislocations should place primary focus on changing the social and economic situations, not the cultural traits of the ghetto underclass. (Wilson 1987, 138)

Drawing upon Wilson's ideas, GEP founders set two goals: first, they created a community institution that could provide human, cultural, and social capital as well as economic opportunities and stability to Sun Valley; second, they sought to interrupt what Wilson identified as "ghetto specific culture" by making visible explicit norms against such behavior via the increased presence of Black female role models. To accomplish the first goal, GEP founders asserted the following:

> Because empowerment is a key concept of GEP, there is a commitment on the part of the organizers to include residents and participants at every level of planning and implementation of the program. This means that adult public housing residents, as well as girls in the targeted age group, will be invited to become members of the governing body. There is also a commitment to training and hiring residents of the neighborhood as staff for the program. The ultimate goal is eventually to turn the operation of the entire program over to public housing residents. (GEP 1992b, 5)

By creating a source of jobs within Sun Valley, GEP sought to directly impact the structural realities within the community as well as provide Sun Valley's

African American women with the skills and expertise necessary to own and operate the program. In this way, the organization was conceptualized as a vehicle for tenant employment and community empowerment.

Despite this lofty goal, GEP struggled for acceptance into the Sun Valley community. Its girls-only policy flew in the face of local and national attention on the "Endangered Black Male." Moreover, its status as an all-female program funded by the Women's Building—often understood as White feminists—prompted criticism that the program caused male/female division within the Black community and perhaps even lesbianism. Drawing upon her community organizing background, Chris, GEP's African American cofounder, met with women in the community. Going door-to-door and talking woman-to-woman, Chris quieted the homophobic whispers and challenged the Black male academy advocates. Because of her efforts, African American women in Sun Valley rallied around GEP and gave the program their support.

The promise of potential employment and eventual resident ownership of the organization successfully countered the naysayers and secured GEP's acceptance into the Sun Valley community. Moreover, as a result of Chris's efforts, Sun Valley women came to see that GEP was real and committed to the community. Roxanne, a former Sun Valley resident and GEP's administrative director, recalled:

> I think they (the parents) settled down and realized that we weren't going to be scared out of here and we were real with what we wanted to do with these girls and they accepted GEP, because there are so many organizations that have come out here to use the community as sources of funding and go on their way. When they realized that GEP was committed to this community, no matter what they did we were going to be here and we were going to be by their side. (age fifty-four)

From the outset, GEP was perceived as a tenant's organization as well as a girl-serving program. Residents were actively involved in the planning stages. Members of the two neighborhood tenant organizations sat on the interim steering committee. Two representatives from the Sun Valley community served as GEP board members. A parent advisory council was created, and early GEP programs included GED classes, Ladies Night, and a Teen Mom's Program. Moreover, to facilitate tenant participation and board member connection to Sun Valley, early board members held all board meetings on site at the bungalow. In fact, this was felt to be so important that "Board meetings will be held on at site at the Bungalow" was written into the organization's bylaws. Overall, GEP was considered a tenant-friendly space and a place where neighborhood women felt their voices would be heard.

True to their word, GEP hired residents as interns or program assistants. Roxanne, the only staff member employed since GEP opened its doors, remembered this:

> Well, when we first started, for every staff member that was a college graduate or professional we had a resident staff person, working alongside that person, hopefully someone that could step into that position. (administrative director, age fifty-four)

In effect, GEP created an "apprenticeship" program. It was the founders' attempt to provide real opportunities for economic and leadership development within the Sun Valley community, thereby improving the community's stability and resiliency. This class agenda was central to the organization's mission.

This initiative, however, was an incredible challenge on many fronts. First, tenant employment strained the capacity of the "professional" staff. As noted earlier, many of the "professional" staff members were young women in their early twenties with only a few years of experience working with youth. These young women were in the process of creating a new program, developing community partnerships, and building relationships with girls—an extraordinary task, even for the most experienced. Yet these young women, many of whom were in their first salaried position at GEP, had little supervisory or job training experience. They were often at a loss regarding how to train the residents, many of whom were mothers in their thirties with little formal youth work training. Navigating the age divide, coupled with the lack of supervisory experience, proved difficult for the young staff.

In addition, there were conflicts regarding resident employees' values and behavior. Roxanne remarked:

> There was a big conflict about some of our residential staff members, and some of their past histories and activities in the communities, and mothers saying, "Oh, no, you have her in there, my daughter is not going to GEP." So the credibility of the residents, in Sun Valley, to be able to teach other girls—the ones that would be credible are not staying in Sun Valley for an eight-hour time, they are going to work. The ones that are here drinking beer sitting on the porch are not necessarily the ones you want teaching your girls. So the plan was a good one, but not realistic. GEP said we would

do trainings and educate them and let them know. There was a resistance by those resident staff members because it was so foreign to their lifestyle, having a drug-free program, carrying yourself in a certain way, they didn't want that change in those ways, they wanted the paycheck, but they didn't want to adapt to GEP rules and regulations. (administrative director, age fifty-four)

Roxanne's insights were unique. As a young woman during the 1960s, she lived in Sun Valley. However, she left Sun Valley and carved out a middle-class lifestyle for her and her family as an executive assistant. When GEP opened its doors, she returned to the community as its administrative director. At the time of my research, she was the only staff member still employed at GEP since the program began. She was the invisible glue that held the program together. From her insider/outsider perspective, many residents did not possess or demonstrate the skill set that GEP required. For example, resident employees were often late and failed to call their supervisor when they were going to miss work. More troubling perhaps was that some resident employees did not possess the core values that GEP wanted to impart to its young charges. As Roxanne recalled, some resident staff hired to work within the program did not always measure up to the community's or organization's ideas of what a decent or good role model should be.

Anderson's (1999) differentiation between "decent" and "street" provides a useful rubric for understanding how distinctions were drawn within Sun Valley as well as GEP. According to Anderson, decent families are those living in poor and working-class communities that still believe a positive future is possible and are committed to middle-class values of hard work, education, and respectability. These families are generally members of the working poor that are integrated into community life via churches and other organizations. Decent parents tend to be considerate of others and strict in their child-rearing practices, and they encourage their children to respect authority (Anderson 1999). Families that Anderson describes as being "street oriented or ghetto," on the other hand, have given up on the "American dream" and have taken on "ghetto-specific culture" as a way of life.

As Roxanne noted in her observations, what set GEP staff and decent tenants apart from those without "credibility as role models" were their performances of middle-class behaviors as represented by sexual respectability, commitment to education, employment, and abstinence from illegal drug use and public intoxication. For many of the newly hired tenants, the separation between their work lives and their private lives disappeared. Drinking, smoking marijuana, experiencing or perpetrating domestic violence, and being "loose, you know, just having lots of men in and out of her house" (Roberta, mother of GEP girl) affected parental approval of GEP and, as a result, girls' attendance. That is, unlike the "professional" staff that may have also engaged in these activities, residents' off-duty activities were community knowledge and dramatically affected their employability. For the resident employees, their lack of class privilege was made real by their inability to leave the office and escape community surveillance and judgment.

Though seldom articulated, these distinctions referenced class tensions that simmered just beneath the surface within GEP. Part of the reason for the silence around such tensions in an organization dedicated to interrupting poverty was that the line between staff and residents or "Us" and "Them" was permeable and changed based upon the criteria put into place. Black class structures do not easily correspond to neat and discrete definitions of class. Instead, class communities within Black society are composed of an "array of incomes, professions and educational levels" (Ginwright 2002, 547). For example, within GEP, staff income ranged from $10,000 a year for part-time staff to upward of $60,000 a year for the executive director. Some parents and caregivers of GEP participants earned $10,000–$15,000 a year, which was as much or more than some direct program staff. In addition, defining class identity was difficult, because individual class identities were not static. For example, several GEP staff members had received government assistance either as youth or young parents prior to their employment at GEP. Finally, the residents of Sun Valley were not a monolithic class community. Several families represented members of the working poor, others were short-term welfare recipients, and still others represented what sociologists have called "the underclass." Despite the difficulty in delineating in concrete terms the class categories, class distinctions were drawn based upon behavior and used to hire and fire employees and grow an organization.

Anderson's (1999) distinctions between decent and street also informed GEP's second goal of decreasing ghetto-specific behavior via the increased presence and visibility of Black female role models. The founders wrote:

> Successful adult role models—real, live people who look like what one will look like when one grows up, and who are successful, productive members of the community—are also critical. Girls growing up in public housing never see, in their day-to-day life, a grown-up who works legitimately and brings home a paycheck. They have no role models suggesting possibilities to which they could aspire. . . . GEP will provide successful adult role models for the girls: African American women who are able to work productively and do not live in poverty. (GEP 1992b, 11)

Despite the obvious exaggerations contained in this assertion, GEP's founders imagined Black women, especially middle-class or professional Black women, serving as real-life examples of "mainstream values pertaining to employment, education, and family structure" (Wilson 1987, 144). They anticipated that these role models would interrupt and challenge the "ghetto-specific culture" and thereby promote employment and self-sufficiency within the community.

In spite of their initial assessment of the structural problems facing poor Black girls, the founders focused their efforts on "exposure" to middle-class cultural values and the creation of a "caring involvement" as the key strategies in promoting poor Black girls' economic mobility and self-sufficiency. Thus rather than create an advocacy program to challenge and change the unequal power relations and resource distribution that underlie poor Black girls' position in the social hierarchy, they created a service program to help individual girls overcome poverty's debilitating effects—"to break the cycle, one girl at a time." Given that the majority of GEP's interim steering committee was composed of service providers, this shift was not surprising. It reflected the founders' pragmatic assessment and belief that this was where they could have the largest impact. The program, while limited in its final scope, represented what they saw as their best effort. In other words, while Wilson's structural analysis provided the founders with an intellectual understanding of the issues facing poor African Americans, their pragmatism and skill set shifted the organization to a service perspective that emphasized cultural interventions. The specific form that such interventions would take was informed by Afrocentric and feminist educational reforms in circulation during this period.

AFROCENTRICITY

Afrocentricity is a critical social theory that holds as its central tenet that "in spite of varying histories, Black societies reflect elements of a core African value system that existed prior to and independently of racial oppression" (Collins 1991, 344; Asante 1988). As a result of this core value system and similar experiences of racial oppression, Black people throughout the Diaspora come to share an Afrocentric consciousness (Collins 1991). During the late 1980s, Afrocentric scholars pointed to the cultural foundation of the public education system as the source of Black youth's poor academic performance, high dropout rates, and resulting status as "Truly Disadvantaged."[2] Afrocentrists charged that within the United States, public education was centered around a Eurocentric cultural foundation that was not only alienating and pushing Black youth out of school but was also grossly miseducating them (Kunjufu 1985; Asante 1990). They asserted that racial pride, which was supported through the use of culturally specific (read race-specific) role models and culturally relevant education, was a key factor in challenging internalized oppression and the low academic achievement of African American children. This time, instead of calling for more resources, teacher testing, or smaller class sizes, critics wanted to change the cultural foundation of education by transforming teacher practices, rewriting student curriculum, and reforming school environments to more appropriately reflect the culture and learning styles of Black youth.

More accurately, they began to address the needs of young Black males or, in the terminology of the day, "The Endangered Black Male." Citing high unemployment and incarceration rates, as well as low rates of high school completion and college attendance for Black boys, proponents argued for the creation of single-sex Black male academies. Geared toward challenging the negative stereotypes Black males encountered and providing a culturally grounded notion of Black masculinity, these academies were to provide a safe space that fostered and motivated learning while raising self-respect, promoting racial and cultural pride, and overcoming obstacles to educational success (Freiberg 1991; Narine 1992). Additionally, with a Black male faculty, these educational initiatives sought to provide students with significant role models and mentors. During 1991 and 1992, at least twenty-two initiatives and proposals were submitted for such academies in cities including Milwaukee, Detroit, New York, Washington, DC, and Baltimore (Ascher 1991).

However, in championing the cause of Black males, Afrocentric activists failed to accurately portray the experiences of Black females. For example, while it was true that Black women had made greater gains relative to White women than had Black men relative to White men, especially in the education and labor markets, Black women barely surpassed Black men in educational achievement, and they still earned less in absolute terms. Black women earned nearly 21 percent less than White men. Afrocentric scholars failed to identify and analyze the persistent patriarchy hidden within the Black woman-to-White woman versus Black man-to-White man comparisons and embedded in Black women's lives.[3]

GEP intended to redirect this "well intentioned but shortsighted response" (GEP 1992b, 3) and focus on Black girls. While Afrocentricity was not written into the original mission statement, the founders noted that "the program was developed within a context of Afrocentric cultural values" (Women's Building 1992). Specifically, Afrocentricity provided GEP founders with a frame for analyzing and addressing racism. The founders wrote:

> Racism communicates to its victims and perpetrators alike that people of color are not as good as white people. In order to overcome the devastating effects of this message, people of color need to learn about the accomplishments of people like themselves throughout history, to counter the image of failure, poverty and victimization. (GEP 1992b, 11)

Within GEP, Afrocentricity was translated into "providing culturally appropriate role models and ethnic history" to foster ethnic pride— a critical source of self-esteem and subsequently a path toward academic and ultimately economic success. Afrocentric educational reforms provided GEP's founders with an ideological framework and model for creating a culturally grounded educational program that celebrated and acknowledged the history and culture of Africans everywhere. In fact, GEP founders asserted that one goal of the program was "to demonstrate the linkage between self-esteem improvement and single-sex, culturally relevant education" (GEP 1992b, 16). Thus the Afrocentric model was institutionalized with the goal to help girls feel better about themselves, so they could resist the devastating effects of racism and achieve within the larger public school system and society at large (GEP 1998). Finally, the connection between safe and separate space with self-esteem and academic achievement resonated with a growing body of feminist scholarship on girls.

FEMINIST CRITIQUES OF EDUCATION

During this same period, scholars of women's psychological development shifted their attention to girls, especially teenage girls (Brown and Gilligan 1990). They asserted that adolescence, that period during which girls are socially scripted to move away from their parents and become women, was a time of heightened psychological risk for girls (Brown and Gilligan 1990). During this time, "girls lose their vitality, their resilience, their immunity to depression, their sense of themselves, and their character" (Brown and Gilligan 1990, 2). They "stop being and start seeming," becoming "female impersonators—separated from their authentic selves and forced to display only their false selves—those selves constructed based upon the answer to the question 'what must I do to please others?' " (Pipher 1994, 21). In other words, during adolescence, young women immersed in a "girl poisoning culture" (Pipher 1994, 21) "realize that men have the power and that their only power comes from consenting to be submissive adored objects" (Pipher 1994, 21).

To document the experiences of girls, the American Association of University Women conducted a national study and found that due to widespread gender bias in the curricula and the classroom, schools were failing girls.[4] Though not without controversy, similar to the Black male academies, single-sex environments were identified as an educational model that could help girls reject limiting gender stereotypes and male dominance as well as reclaim their voice and authentic sense of self.[5] Girl-only academies in the form of single-sex classes within public coed facilities and private girls schools were created and blossomed across the country.

Unfortunately, the feminist educational reforms failed to account for the effects of race on girls' self-esteem. In other words, similar to Afrocentric efforts, feminist educational reforms pushed to the margins the experiences of Black girls. This marginalization maintained the invisibility of Black girls' experiences and resulted in a continued lack of research, programs, and services to appropriately address their needs and concerns. Such implications warranted further scrutiny into this both/and space where African American girls live. The creators of GEP took up this challenge and took a closer look into the lives of Black girls.

GEP founders drew upon the gender research and asserted that "to survive and flourish, girls needed a safe and separate space to overcome the pervasive but unconscious sexism that perpetuate[s] girls' low self-esteem, poor achievement, and low aspirations" (GEP 1992b, 13). Specifically, the founders hoped to "demonstrate to girls that they have the same potential as boys—making up for gender inequalities in youth programming and the sexism of the school system, which reinforce the message that girls are second-class citizens, can't achieve as much as boys, and require male approval for their self esteem" (16).Within this refuge, the young women can "learn that battering and abuse are never justified; how to take care of their bodies; and how not to become pregnant" (13). Thus the goal of the program was not to

> separate them [the participants] from males but rather to get them healthier and stronger in their own self-esteem in relation to men and therefore have a better chance of creating strong family and relational bonds. (GEP 1992b, 13)

The program was designed to help young women become strong, empowered heterosexual women and mothers. The goal was to strengthen the young women so that they could become successful within mainstream society.

Overall, GEP's founding ideologies contained goals of equal access and individual empowerment thought to be achieved via feminist and Afrocentric strategies of culturally relevant, and separate, programming. Sheltered from a racist and "girl-poisoning culture," girls would be "exposed" to ethnic- and gender-specific cultural enrichment as well as middle- and working-class African American women who served as mentors and role models. As a result of this race- and gender-specific education and mentorship, girls would experience an increase in racial and gender pride and thus an increase in self-esteem, academic achievement, labor market participation, and, most importantly a decrease in teen pregnancy. These tenets represent the ideological roots of GEP and subsequently the foundation for its organizational culture of empowerment.

GEP'S EMERGENT CULTURE OF EMPOWERMENT

> GEP is an important part of my life. I love to come to GEP because the people there care for us and help us when we need help. (Christa, GEP girl, age ten)

As noted earlier, both scholars and activists have called for the creation of safe spaces for women and girls to "try on ways of being women." While the word "safe" is used freely, it begs the questions: Safe from what? Safe from whom? At a basic level of understanding, "safe space" within GEP translated to women and girls being both literally and figuratively safe—safe from physical, emotional, and social harm. Within GEP, this was not taken lightly. Ten-year-old Mekka wrote this:

> Dear Alice Walker
> . . . GEP is a great place; they teach me things about body parts and hygiene. My life is important to me and being safe is important to me. . . .
> I live in Sun Valley. It is not that bad in Sun Valley, but sometimes there is shooting. Someone just got shot in the head. I don't feel safe when there is violence; I feel scared. I want to feel calm whenever I feel scared . . . I want a safe life without violence. I don't want to live around violence when I grow up. Violence is when there are drug addicts around and when there is shooting, kidnapping and fighting. You can get killed by fighting. I want to live around nice grass, beautiful flowers and intelligent people. Not all people who are raised in the ghetto end up being violent. They can end up being respectful, they don't call people names and they don't have guns. I want violent people to stop because they can get in trouble and go to jail, kill people and make people feel unsafe. . . .
> I admire you Alice Walker. . . . You are a free woman in this world. (GEP girl)

GEP opened its doors during the height of Bay City's neighborhood drug wars over crack cocaine distribution. During this period, Sun Valley, also known as "the Swamp," had the reputation of being the most violent and dangerous neighborhood in the city. In fact, during GEP's first summer, five homicides occurred in the neighborhood. During these early days, GEP staff and girls had "drive-by drills" to be ready when gunshots were heard. Unfortunately, there was no need for practice; drive-bys were a frequent occurrence, during which girls and staff "assumed the position."

But random violence, although real and rampant, represented only one part of these young women's dangerous realities. Staff also assisted girls in making personal safety plans. Fighting between adults, especially their mothers and their partners, as well as the girls' own safety within their homes, was a serious issue. In addition, girls had to navigate "the streets," and, for GEP girls, this was often accomplished through fighting. As thirteen-year-old Tori noted: "Some of the stuff that starts happening to girls at my school is they start having fights over 'he say, she say' stuff. I know that to be true because it has happened to me" Girls *had to* fight at home, at school, in the streets. They had to "watch their backs" and "keep an eye on the haters," those "people who try to tear you down when you are trying to make something of yourself" (Tori, GEP girl, age thirteen). In the midst of this, GEP explicitly set about constructing a place with "beautiful flowers" as a temporary escape from these dangers for a small part of the day.

Within GEP, "safe space" also represented an environment that was open and allowed for an exchange of ideas and an exploration of different points of view—a space that allowed girls and staff to form their own ideas and to learn to stand their own ground. Group, that space within the organization where the girls and staff met to discuss issues affecting their lives, put these ideas of safety into practice. Group was the heart of GEP and its program curriculum, and GEP founders actively integrated group into the program's daily curriculum. In the founders' original program proposal, they asserted this:

> Every day there will be a women's support group meeting to address health education issues and peer problems, such as rape, pregnancy, sex and safe sex, racism, homophobia, substance abuse, mother-daughter relationships, violence, boys, AIDS, gossip, school problems, African American history/culture, "street law," assertiveness training, domestic violence education, sexual identity, conflict resolution, budget development and money management, grooming, nutrition, etc. (GEP 1992b, 14)

Group was the place in the program where consciousness-raising occurred and girls' voices and experiences were recognized and valued. It was the space where safety was intentionally and explicitly created and maintained. Consider the following observation:

As the time draws nearer to 4 [p.m.], Maya begins to round up Group B, or the 11-to-14-year-olds. The girls, still chatting about the drama of the day and finishing their snack, begin to congregate in the "chill-out room." The first girls in grab seats on the couch, and the others loudly move their chairs to face the couch, rounding out into a small circle. There are new girls in the group today. It appears that most of the group members know the new girls from school or the neighborhood; still, Maya begins by asking the new girls to introduce themselves. Quickly, glancing around the circle, with her knees pulled in and her chin pressed against her chest, the first girl introduces herself as Alisha. She's been to GEP before, but it was awhile ago and she was in the younger group with a different coordinator. The second girl, Alisha's friend from school, introduces herself as Anna.

Maya takes this opportunity to review the group's ground rules or agreements. She asks for volunteers. The girls reply. "The first rule is respect." From the tone of their voices and their energy, I get the sense that this is important and that they've done this many times! "One person talks at a time." "Confidentiality or what you see in here, say in here, stays in here" another explains. "No put downs, or no dissin' or cappin on each other." Maya points to the rules listed on a poster hanging on the wall. She asks Anna and Alisha if they have any questions or if they have any rules to add to the group. Both say no. She explains that the reason for the ground rules is to make it safe for people to say what's on their mind and what they're feeling without being worried that it will get back to other people, or that they will be made fun of. She asks the new girls if they can agree to abide by the rules; they say yes. With the ground rules in place, check-in begins. (Field notes)

Drawing upon support group notions of community agreements, GEP coordinators worked with the girls to create a space that was safe from rejection and ridicule and that would facilitate feelings of respect and sisterhood. The "safety" rules constructed for group were not limited only to group time but were posted around the space and constantly referred to throughout the day. In this way, group set into motion an explicit practice of safety, trust, and respect that developed into an overall characteristic of the organization's climate.

Group signaled for the women and girls that GEP was a different place. "Hatin' " and "haters" were not tolerated. Fighting and name calling or cappin' were not allowed, and strict rules and consequences were developed to deal with such behavior. Stall and Stoecker (1998) found that women use small groups to establish trust and build relationships. These small groups create an atmosphere that affirms each participant's contribution, provides the time for individuals to share, and helps participants listen carefully to each other. Moreover, smaller group settings create and sustain the relationship building and sense of significance and solidarity so integral to community. (Stall and Stoecker 1998, 746).

Group and the agreements had a profound effect on the way GEP's space was imagined and perceived by the women and girls. It facilitated the development of a community grounded in safety, trust, respect, and, ultimately, empowerment.

As a result, GEP became a space that women and girls called home. bell hooks (1990) writes:

Historically African American people believed that the construction of a homeplace, however fragile and tenuous (the slave hut, the wooden shack), had a radical political dimension . . . it was about the construction of a safe place where Black people could affirm one another and by so doing begin . . . healing the wounds inflicted by racist domination. (42)

Homeplaces are spaces that provide shelter from both dominant and indigenous oppression and marginalization and create the conditions in which Black women and girls can connect and self-affirm. Nyema reflected:

I've been in GEP since the program started, and this is definitely my second home. This—GEP would be the first place, like if I ever was in a crisis, if I ever got beat, you know, God forbid, and I know that I would not be able to tell my mother. GEP would be the next mother that I would tell. They've been that mother. When I can't go to mom, when we're not OK, whenever something happens they're there. And they supported my learning and my choices when other Black women, who I guess are my peers, looked at me and said, "You think you are all that. You think you too good. We don't want you to be Black. We don't want you to be a part of us, because you think you are all that. You doin' too much." And GEP took me in and said, "Naw, naw, you just be Nyema, you know. Don't worry about the rest. We got it." (GEP girl and intern, age seventeen)

GEP was Nyema's second home, a place that allowed her to "just be Nyema," despite others and especially Black women's rejection. GEP was a safe place where Nyema and the other Black girls who participated in the program could be "connected to each other and to their inner selves" (Pastor, McCormick and Fine 1996).

GEP's discourse of empowerment, while problematic in its articulation, provided an opportunity for women and girls to construct a homeplace. This homeplace had profound effects for what happened once the women and girls entered the organization. That is, although the founders' ideologies were important for structuring the creation of the program, it was not until the women and girls brought the organization "to life" that the culture of the organization began to emerge. Staff and girls latched onto the discourse of empowerment and made GEP a safe (or, rather, safer) place. A key illustration of this culture in practice was the revision of the organization's mission statement.

STRONG GIRLS → POWERFUL WOMEN

GEP, in 1996, took on the motto "Strong Girls→Powerful Women" and revised its mission statement to read:

> GEP enables girls who live in public housing to access their power to lead productive lives. GEP promotes girls' self-sufficiency, self-determination, leadership development, and conflict management skills: improves their self-esteem; inspires learning and vision; and enhances health, family wellness, and the notion of "giving back." GEP works within an Africentric womanist context, and is grounded in accountability to the community. (GEP 1998, 1)

As noted earlier, implicit in the founding mission statement was a representation of GEP girls as "Urban Girls." Defined as "at-risk," GEP girls needed to be fixed. With the construction of the new mission statement, however, GEP ushered in "The Strong Black Girl." This figure, while still drawing upon the plight of poor Black girls surviving in urban ghettos, highlighted the girls' strength, resiliency, courage, and power. Central to the new shift in direction was the adoption of youth development principles.

YOUTH DEVELOPMENT

Youth development represents a movement away from an "at-risk" framework to one that draws upon youths' potential. Specifically, it can be defined as the ongoing growth process in which all youth are engaged in attempting to (1) meet their basic personal and social needs to be safe, feel cared for, be valued, be useful, and be spiritually grounded, and (2) to build skills and competencies that allow them to function and contribute in their daily lives. (Pittman, O'Brien, and Kimball 1993, 8)

Drawing upon youth development discourse, Ife suggested that GEP attempted to move "from a deficit to an asset" perspective and started to see the girls not in terms of problems but potential. Ife recalled:

Remember "Ghetto Personality Disorder"! We were constantly attaching a problem, creating a sense of what the girls could not do into our writing. It took a lot to make the shift. (executive director, age thirty-six)

Key to this change was the phrase "enable girls to access their power." Ife, the then-newly hired executive director, in close conversation with the board of directors, was pivotal regarding this change. She wrote:

Enable vs. Empower! This was an interesting debate. We defined empower as giving someone power . . . allowing them to be in control—that if it wasn't for us they wouldn't be able to do anything. It was defined as we were going to find the power, the authority, the approval, for them to be engaged—versus enabling them to see for themselves that they could do anything. We were going to give them the tools, the opportunities, the space to really test out their own sense of what was correct, what they believed they should be doing. They would be allowed to make mistakes in this process of being able. Enabling for us suggested that girls already had the power and our job was only to help them uncover it. (age thirty-six)

The move from "empower" to "enable" was significant and shifted the organizational imagination such that Black girls were no longer seen as powerless victims. It was a move from "giving someone power" to a concept of enabling, which "suggested that the girls already had the power." Thus the goal was to help the young women "uncover" their own power that had been denied them or silenced due to their structural location and lived experiences. With the discursive move to "enable," GEP was attempting to move beyond this limited conception of empowerment to a real place and practice of power sharing. But this move was not without complications. As Ife noted:

Mind you, "enabling" was not the best thing either. That generally meant you were letting someone have their way to do negative behaviors, but they couldn't do it if you weren't there in some way helping them. (executive director, age thirty-six)

Rather than "giving power," GEP women were conceptualized as bridges with the resources or "the tools, the opportunities, the space" for girls to self-actualize—"to really test out their own sense of what was correct, what they believed they should be doing."
According to Ife, "enable" also

meant giving up some power, that the girls would be made partners in the very beginning of the process to assist them to access their sense of self, be inspired to learn, understand themselves culturally. (executive director, age thirty-six)

Thus the use of the term *enable* pushed GEP staff to make two significant leaps in their understanding regarding power. First, this shift acknowledged that Black girls had power. Second, it also made clear that Black women also had power—power they simultaneously claimed for themselves and then "gave up" when working with the girls. The Africentric womanist context was imagined as a pivotal space wherein such work could occur.

THE AFRICENTRIC WOMANIST
CONTEXT DEFINED

As noted earlier, Afrocentricity and feminism were key organizing principles in creating GEP. However, while both terms were incorporated into the organization's first funding proposal, they were not included in the original mission statement. With the new mission statement, Afrocentricity and womanism became codified and the Africentric womanist perspective explained.

In preparation for staff development training on the core values and mission of the organization, Ife wrote the following:

I will try to give you the framework for Africentric thought within GEP.
1. Within GEP we give ourselves permission to acknowledge the Creator in the work that we do. . . . Girls are encouraged to see GOD within themselves, let GOD shine within them (it's on the walls).

2. We teach a reverence for Ancestors: we learn the history/ herstory of Africans in this country, we encourage them to create sacred spaces for their ancestors, we pour libation.

3. We acknowledge Elders. There is clearly a place for the parents—we want to hear their voice. We open our space to invite elders and folks from the community to share things about their lives with the girls. We hope we can learn lessons from their lives, hear their wisdom.

4. We respect Children. We acknowledge them as our wealth and health within the community. We place some expectations on them, hold them responsible for their learning, create opportunities for them to excel, honor their presence and wisdom—realizing that they are closest to the Most High.

5. We have a respect within GEP for the male and female principle. . . . We seek to nurture all of those that are within the community. We open our doors to the boys; we invite men in our program to be strong models for our girls, to learn how to respect female energy. We teach girls to honor the strength and value of the female principle—understand its properties.

6. Reflection: Know Thy Self—GEP values reflection, we ask everyone to be open to this process. We ask the girls and the parents. We call it critical thinking. We ask for their opinion, we ask them to evaluate everything that goes on in the program. We ask everyone to work on themselves. We ask them to journal, to meditate, to learn to listen to their voice within. We have also realized the importance of creating this opportunity amongst staff. (executive director, age thirty-six)

I quote Ife extensively because her understanding and articulation of Afrocentricity served as the foundation for organizational trainings and set into motion the practice of the organization's new vision. With the presentation of these six principles, Ife attempted to outline the organization's "Africentric" ideology regarding spirituality, male-female relationships, community roles and responsibilities, and self as manifested in the organization's youth work and practices. Though many women had heard of Afrocentricity, it was not until they became GEP employees and participated in a training dedicated to the discussion of the philosophy that these six principles became incorporated into their own understanding of the term.

When asked what "Afrocentric" meant, staff reflected:

Knowledge. Knowing there is nothing wrong with being Black. (Yasmine, program coordinator, age thirty)

Teaching the heritage, history, and ancestry to the young people. Teach them who we are as a people. (Aisha, program coordinator, age twenty-four)

Before I came here I heard about Afrocentric, but I didn't know how it applied to women. I think it's been more around traditions and holidays, but not really incorporating them into our everyday lives, like the values of it, so I think that here we are definitely striving for, not just to make it OK or affirm and validate it during celebrations, but to make those principles of how we are living and healthy living to realize the importance of faith and spirituality and parts of creativity in terms of how resourceful we are. (Jamila, program assistant, age twenty)

Afrocentric to me means basically that which is African-centered, in terms of culturally derived from Africa—derived, and not necessarily directly African, but culturally derived, spiritually derived, emotionally derived from Africa in terms of—and Africa is broad, because we're talking about a continent of, of many, many different peoples and many different principles, but that—there's an overall sense, an African sense of community and respect for elders, respect for the ancestors, a worship and respect for the earth and all—and that the earth sustains us, that we belong to it, it does not belong to us. (Ananda, dance instructor, age thirty-five)

GEP girl and program intern Nyema remembers how she came to learn about Afrocentricity. She recounted:

It was through just a typical, typical program . . . and through that I took on the meaning, which to me is to be one who is grounded in their history, that history of course being African. One who is able to—I don't want to say blend, but one who is able to have their historical parts and modern parts of themselves work cohesively. So like the part of us that is now, working with what was before us and the connection that we're a part of, and to be proud of that. I think that's Afrocentricity itself. Its whole essence is in pride. (age seventeen)

Afrocentricity was embedded within the organization's service and advocacy work. Perhaps the best example of this ideology in practice was the annual Kwanzaa celebration.[6] While the community Kwanzaa celebration was only one evening, the celebration represented more than three months of preparation and a large percentage of GEP's financial resources. In preparation for and during the event, GEP women and girls explicitly incorporated the six Africentric elements, as outlined by Ife, into daily organizational life. During this period, libation, an African tradition of honoring the Creator and the Ancestors, was explained and poured. The Nguzo Saba, or guiding principles of Kwanzaa, was taught, remembered, and brought to life through skits and songs.[7] Elders and children were acknowledged and honored for their particular roles in the development of Bay City's and, in particular, Sun Valley's, Black communities. Girls drummed, sang traditional African songs, and performed traditional African dances as well as contemporary hip-hop routines.

In honor of this yearly community celebration, eleven-year-old Kendra wrote:

CELEBRATING KWANZAA

I like when we're
all singing and dancing.
We have very loud voices.
We hear all kinds of sounds
like clapping, stomping our feet,
drums, birimbau, cowbells
and stuff like that.
We sing capoeira songs.
We do hip-hop dancing,
like the leg pop and the tick tock
you know
stuff like that.

Girls also wrote and performed plays about HIV and AIDS, tackling in the process male-female relationships, sexuality, homophobia, domestic violence, and family issues. Kwanzaa in many ways represented an explicit ongoing commitment and community sharing of GEP's Africentric perspective. It encouraged GEP women and girls to not only connect as Blacks, Africans, and African Americans, and to be knowledgeable and proud of their African and African American past, but also to reconnect as present-day Sun Valley residents.

Yet while Ife's articulation of GEP's Africentric perspective built upon tenets of Afrocentric ideology, it also contained significant differences. For example, within Afrocentric ideology, scholars assert that African Americans share a cultural sensibility rooted in African cultural values and traditions that transcend time and place—thus reducing African culture to a static "essence" rather than expanding culture to be a dynamic and fluid process embedded in lived realities.[8] As a result, Afrocentricity is organized around a race-first ideology that suppresses differences and divisions, especially gender inequality, within its own "imagined community." To counter these limitations, Ife modified Afrocentricity's gender ideology and articulated an Africentric womanist perspective.

While more recent writings on womanism exist today, GEP staff, without fail, drew upon the work of Alice Walker. In her book *In Search of Our Mothers' Gardens*, Walker (1983) introduces and defines the concept and politics of womanism. She writes:

> From Womanish (opposite of "girlish," i.e., frivolous, irresponsible, not serious). A black feminist or feminist or feminist of color . . . usually referring to outrageous, audacious, courageous or willful behavior. . . .
>
> Also woman who loves other women, sexually and/or nonsexually. Appreciate and prefers women's culture . . . and women's strength. . . . Committed to survival and wholeness of entire people, male and female. . . . Loves music, Loves dance, Loves the moon, Loves the Spirit. . . . Loves struggle. Loves the folk. Loves herself. *Regardless*.
>
> Womanist is to feminist, like purple is to lavender. (xi–xii)

Walker brought a racialized lens to feminism and linked Black women's activism with their history and experience of enslavement and freedom. In contrast to feminism, Walker addressed Black women's commitment to their communities and their fight not only against gender but race and class oppression. In addition, she addressed Black women's and girls' spirituality, as well as their "outrageous, audacious, courageous or willful behavior."

It was this understanding of womanism that permeated GEP. At a GEP staff training retreat, when asked what womanist meant to them, staff responded:

> I heard womanist from Alice Walker, I read all of her stuff and love the term womanist . . . because it included love and beauty in a way that feminism never did for me. I would say I'm a feminist, womanist, but I like womanist better, because it embraces more of the spirit. And I don't feel that in feminism at all. (Danielle, program coordinator, age twenty-six)

> It means we have a female-centered and focused approach and vision, that we pay attention to the thinking and emotions of women. This is about shifting the paradigm and not thinking about this like a male would. (Maya, program coordinator, age twenty-three)

We are women-focused but not male-exclusive. (Yasmine, program coordinator, age thirty)

It operates on several levels: (1) Empowering young women, teaching them that they can have the tools they need. (2) Womanist is about how we work together. We are different from men. To recognize and honor that difference. (3) Putting our voice out. Letting the community know that we are there and available for women and girls, invite them to come to us for information. Checking out where girls are in a political, almost antagonistic way. (Ife, executive director, age thirty-six)

That we are here to help girls and that we help them (and ourselves) understand our power. (Aisha, program coordinator, age twenty-four)

I think that in my upbringing and education I've heard it [feminism] to be more associated with White upper-class women and didn't really take ownership of it. I knew what it was to be a woman, a Black woman . . . and womanist incorporates that identity and realizes it's not separate. You're not just Black and you're not just a woman, but you're both . . . I'm working on and helping the girls to realize . . . all the perspectives we can bring as Black women, helping them understand they have a voice in that. Helping them articulate it—you know what it means to be Black and you know what it means to be a girl, and how your experience is unique and different. (Cheryl, program coordinator, age twenty-five)

Most understood womanism as a certain level of support, understanding, and common ground that women shared. It was understood as Black feminism—as love for Black women and commitment to the struggle for Black women's and the Black community's liberation.

Importantly, within GEP, Africentricity and womanism were rarely spoken of separately. By bringing together the terms *Africentric* and *womanist*, GEP made visible and honored African and African American cultures and articulated an understanding of womanhood, especially a liberated version of womanhood, as racially embedded, connected to the entire community, and encompassing "beauty," "spirituality," and a "celebration of women's creative energy."[9] Africentric womanism created a space where Black women and girls could explore their voices, their choices, and their power.

Perhaps the most compelling example of Africentric womanism in practice was GEP's Black Herstory Celebration. This annual event occurred at the beginning of March and simultaneously highlighted Black women's and girls' both/and status as well as critiqued their exclusion during many Black History and Women's History Months' celebrations. This celebration of Black womanhood often included girls' original poetry as well as performances of well-known womanist poems such as "Phenomenal Woman" and "Still I Rise" by Maya Angelou. Thirteen-year-old Alisha, for example, wrote and performed the following:

> BEAUTIFUL AND BLACK
>
> Black and beautiful,
> Yeah that's me.
> Black and beautiful,
> That's, what you can call me.
> Average-type hair,
> Don't judge me from the things that I wear.
> Don't say smart words
> Because I don't care.
> Girl, go and put your hair
> In any way you want to wear it
> Well, I'm not the one who can tell you
> When and where to do something
> Because it is your choice.
> I am Black and beautiful
> Because that is what I want to be called . . .

The revision of GEP's mission and the inclusion of Africentric womanism into the organizational culture had a profound impact on the women's and girls' identity work. Most importantly, the revision itself was a form of identity work. By challenging and replacing "The Urban Girl" with "The Strong Girl," GEP women altered the discursive terrain within the organization as well as challenged negative representations of Black girlhood. However, not all changes in the mission statement were as progressive.

GROUNDED IN ACCOUNTABILITY TO THE COMMUNITY

The revision of the mission statement also shifted the relationship between the organization and Sun Valley's African American community. At the outset, GEP focused on tenant employment as a means to community empowerment and, ultimately, community ownership of the program. With the new mission, however, tenant empowerment was replaced by the notion of being "grounded in accountability to the community." According to board retreat documents and interviews with board members, the change was necessary so the organization could become more focused on its work with the girls. While this may be the case, the overall impact of change shifted the ownership of the program from Sun Valley residents and placed it squarely within the hands of the staff.

This change in ownership brought to the fore several unresolved class tensions between GEP and the Sun Valley community. While power had always been in the hands of the professional women, at the outset there was a conscious effort to share and even transfer this power to community residents. With the new mission, this more progressive class agenda became muted, and distinctions between the organization and the community became hardened. One potential explanation for this shift was the organizational realities of GEP. The tenant employment program, while a great idea on paper, was a challenge to properly manage. Finding staff competent in both youth development and adult employment development was difficult. Moreover, navigating the complex "decent" and "street" distinctions within the community created hiring conflicts and impacted the girls' attendance.

Another explanation for the shift might lay with the adoption of Afrocentricity as an ideological foundation for the organization. Ginwright (2002), drawing upon an in-depth case study of Afrocentric educational reform in West Oakland, California, suggests that Afrocentricity, by claiming that poor and working-class blacks must reclaim their original African identity, values, and culture and then they will be successful, brings along its very own culture of poverty thesis. Though GEP did not adopt such a strong Afrocentric frame, its Afrocentric and perhaps even womanist philosophies identified ideal practices and values that may or may not correspond to those practiced among Sun Valley residents.

In reflecting on the change, Ife wrote:

> You know there were still people of the mind-set that the agency was going to be turned over to the community in three years and that was really important. It wasn't until a year or so later [after the revision of the mission] I could engage community because they [the community] weren't accountable or responsible for the program. (Executive director, age thirty-six)

While the underlying cause for the change can be debated, in practice, the change had real implications for GEP's daily programming and community relations. This move from tenant empowerment to "accountability to the community" was matched by a shift in organizational resources from the adult women within Sun Valley community to the girls. The GED classes and Ladies Night programs were cancelled, and the organization's relationships with the tenant advisory board and resident council deteriorated. No new residents were recruited as board members, and board meetings began to be held off site. It was not that the community was not important—it was just that community *development* was not as important as an individual girl's success.

In sum, both GEP's original and current mission statements supported the development of a space for Black women and girls to "empower" themselves. In this chapter, I suggested that GEP's founders, drawing upon the race, class, and gender reforms of the period, developed an organizational culture based upon an ideology of empowerment. The program's founders subsequently identified "exposure" to working- and middle-class African American women, ethnic and gender pride, self-esteem, academic achievement, and vocational exploration as strategies for improved economic outcomes for girls rather than altering the economic and political structures, such as capitalism, that created conditions. As a result, GEP founders structured the program around group.

Group became the key to GEP's organizational identity and culture of empowerment. It was here that safety was created and constructed. Moreover, it was within group that girls explored alternative femininities and masculinities as well as challenged race, class, and gender inequalities. Group facilitated the construction of GEP as a safe space where girls and women could become empowered.

One result of this culture of empowerment was the revision of GEP's mission statement. Within this process, GEP women redefined and represented not only the organization but themselves and the girls they served, transforming "The Urban Girl" into "A Strong Black Girl." In other words, in revisioning the organizational mission to explicitly include Africentric womanism, GEP women drew upon the cultural discourse of empowerment to assert their autonomous and powerful identities. This discourse further opened the space for Black women and girls to locate themselves within their own herstory and traditions to create meaningful and powerful identities.

Yet empowerment is not always what it seems. The incorporation of Africentric womanism also shifted the organization's class perspective and seemed to push to the fore middle-class perspectives and priorities. Key to the study of empowerment is an exploration of how different sources of power circulate in various social contexts. That is, it not enough to assume "empowerment" based upon shared social identities or good intentions, and likewise to assume disempowerment and marginalization because of differing race, class, or gender identities. Instead, we must look to larger patterns of power relations as well as those shaped and framed by the organizational context. These patterns will be discussed in the next chapter.

4

GEP's Organizational Structure and Power Matrix

Organizational structure delineates how power is formally structured to move within an organization (Tayeb 1988). Hall (1987) suggests that "organizational structure is analogous to the structure of a building; just as walls, floors, and ceilings influence and constrain our interactions so too does organizational structure" (56). Specifically, it serves to define the organizational hierarchy and make clear decision-making processes and procedures. Yet organizational structure can and does change. Similar to organizational culture, it "evolves as a consequence of the activities that take place within it" (Hall 1987, 56).

Given the role of organizational structure in shaping power dynamics, it has been a hotly debated topic within feminist circles. Most early discussions of women's organizing and organizations either articulated what was wrong with bureaucracy or argued the fundamental incompatibility between bureaucracy and feminism (Kornegger 1975; Browne 1976; Rothschild 1976; Ferguson 1984).[1] Recently, scholars have found that women have created hybrid organizations that blend characteristics from collective and bureaucratic forms.[2] Bordt (1997), for example, found that 75 percent of women's nonprofit organizations in New York were a hybrid form. Furthermore, she noted that organizations composed of, or working with, minority (oppressed) populations tended to adopt a hybrid form.

Sudbury (1998) also found hybrid structures within Black women's organizations. In particular, she noted that Black women's organizations shared "an organic commitment to the creation of empowering structures and avoidance of top-down decision making," which did not necessarily evolve into "overtly feminist models of organizing" (133). Rather, within these spaces, "the ideals of empowerment and equality coexisted comfortably alongside the need for leadership" (133). In other words, within Black women's organizations, empowerment was not equated with collectivism, and hierarchy was not equated with oppression. Instead, she suggests the following:

> Black women are in fact tuning into a far more nuanced under-standing of power, a discourse which recognizes its "two faces." Rather than rejecting all over manifestations of power, they attempt to balance the need to oppose abuses of power with the desire to enable women to experience control and authority. (Sudbury 1998, 135)

It seems that Black women incorporate both hierarchical and collective strategies into their organizing and organizations to create opportunities for women to share power collectively, as well as to be in positions of authority and thus to learn how to use power in a liberating and transformative fashion.

In this chapter, I explore GEP's organizational structure and power matrix. I suggest that GEP founders created a hybrid organization structured along both bureaucratic and collective ideals. Its bureaucratic or hierarchical tendencies reflected the discourse of control found within its organizational environment, while the discourse of empowerment promoted more collec-tivist tendencies toward consensus building and power-sharing practices. These contradictory impulses created an ambiguous power structure within GEP that was most clearly manifested in the organization's decision-making practices. Most of the time, empowerment took precedence over control within GEP. For example, as noted in the previous chapter, the discourse of empowerment opened up a space for GEP women to revise the organization's mission and shift the organization from a teen pregnancy prevention pro-gram to a youth development organization grounded in an Africentric wom-anist context.

Yet empowerment also took the form of resisting organizational author-ity. For example, GEP women drew upon the discourse of sisterhood to chal-lenge organizational policies and power relationships. GEP girls, drawing upon the youth development discourse and their status as consumers, spoke up, spoke out, walked in, and walked out within the context of GEP. This hybrid structure, in conjunction with GEP's environment and culture, com-bined to create an organizational power matrix that opened up space for both women and girls to "do power." It became a social space that interrupted and oftentimes altered the terrain of power and voice that the staff and partici-

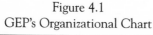

Figure 4.1
GEP's Organizational Chart

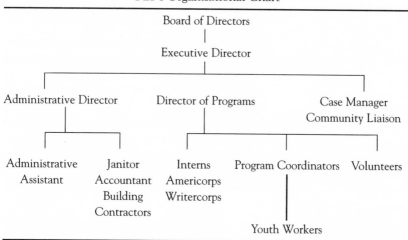

pants experienced in their daily lives. This organizational power matrix served as the springboard for the participants' identity work.

GEP'S FORMAL ORGANIZATIONAL STRUCTURE

GEP was a five-tiered organization. Similar to other bureaucratic service organizations, GEP had a formal hierarchical structure with highly specified written rules and formal social controls. The job positions within the organization were not temporary or rotating but permanent placements with job descriptions. While staff configurations within GEP have varied over time, these variations did not significantly alter the organization's underlying structure.

The board of directors, which ranged from four to six members during the research period, represented the first tier. Though often invisible, this volunteer board, composed of teachers, health educators, lawyers, real estate agents, and nonprofit grant makers, was the legal and visioning body of the organization. Meeting once a month as a whole board and as necessary on various committees, the board worked in collaboration with and supervised the executive director to ensure the success of the organization. The board conceptualized its role as "supporting the Executive Director by helping set policy, brainstorming new ideas, giving suggestions and advice when solicited, and helping with special events or projects" (as quoted in Gamble and Associates 1999, 4). The board's helping perspective minimized its role at the top of the organizational hierarchy and shifted power to Ife, the exec-utive director. Thus while she occupied the second rung, she was the most powerful.

Ife was the driving force of the organization. She was the public face of the organization and was responsible for carrying out the vision and mission in the day-to-day operation of the program, as well as securing the necessary funds for the program to operate. Ife worked closely with the administrative, or management, team. This team consisted of three women in addition to the executive director: the administrative director, the director of programs, and at times a case manager or community outreach coordinator. During their weekly meetings, the administrative team worked in conjunction with the executive director to coordinate all areas of the organization and to ensure that "the left hand knew what the right hand was doing" (Roxanne, administrative director). This team was created so that the organization, as represented through management, would be of one mind with regard to orga-nizational vision, programmatic implementation, and staff policies.

Program and support staff comprised the fourth rung on the organiza-tional hierarchy. The program team consisted of three to seven women responsible for providing direct service to the girls, as well as volunteers and interns. The support team consisted of one bookkeeper and a janitor. While both janitorial and bookkeeping services were important to GEP's smooth functioning, the program team occupied a more central role in GEP's daily functioning and identity. The program coordinators were the face of the organization to the girls and parents within Sun Valley. That is, while Ife was the public face to funders and other community and neighborhood groups, the program coordinators represented the individual faces that girls, parents, and even teachers came to know and with whom they interacted on a daily basis. Most important, the program coordinators were responsible for the day-to-day delivery and implementation of the program's mission.

Volunteers and interns were also members of the program team. While both volunteers and interns occupied the same tier, interns were much more central to the daily functioning of the organization. Interns, which included those hired by the organization as well as those brought into the organization through programs such as Americorps and WritersCorps, worked between ten and twenty hours a week with the program coordinators.[3] Interns did not simply "help out" but became members of the program team supported and supervised by the program coordinators. They were expected to develop their own programs and relationships with the girls. Volunteers, on the other hand, generally came in once or twice a week and helped out. Volunteers were not responsible for disciplining the girls. Rather, coordinators were expected to keep order and a respectful atmosphere.

GEP girls occupied a shifting and somewhat complicated position within the organizational hierarchy. They were clients and consumers of GEP's services as well as temporary employees. For example, at various points in its history, GEP employed program participants via a city-operated youth employment program. As youth workers, GEP girls age thirteen and older were hired to assist with administrative and program activities. They were also hired as interns. GEP interns were at least seventeen years old and also had more responsibility than the youth workers. As interns, they were in charge of leading a particular program within the organization. For example, Nyema and Monica, both GEP interns, worked as the coordinator/facilitator of the NIA collective.

GEP girls were also clients and consumers of GEP's services. As clients they were closely supervised and subjected to disciplinary actions from interns, coordinators, the administrative team, the executive director, and board members. In this location, the girls were "subordinate" to all "adults" in the organization. However, as will be discussed in detail later in the chapter, the girls were also constructed as, and constructed themselves as, consumers. As consumers, the girls were simultaneously inside and outside agents whose choices fundamentally shaped GEP's future. From this perspective they were not subordinate to all adults but, rather, exercised a considerable amount of power within the organization.

Despite this seemingly straightforward top-down structure, power moved in unexpected ways within GEP. At times the top-down hierarchy overrode the culture of empowerment. At other times, the culture of empowerment toppled the formal hierarchy. Most often, staff and girls experienced confusion and opportunities. Examining GEP's decision-making practices makes both the confusion and opportunities more visible.

GEP'S DECISION-MAKING PRACTICES

In organizational studies a key differentiating characteristic between collective and bureaucratic organizations is the decision-making process: bureaucracies emphasize top-down decision making and power as domination and control, whereas collectives emphasize participatory decision making and power conceptualized as empowerment (Rothschild-Whitt 1979; Bordt 1997). Recently, scholars have noted that power comes from other sources and moves through channels other than the formal decision-making structure (Hall 1987). However, the decision-making structure, or how decisions are to be made, does set into place the "formal" structure around which an informal structure and alternative decision-making strategies are constructed. Thus it is important to clarify the "formal" structure.

Within GEP, decision making was both a process determined by one's position in the organizational hierarchy and a collective process based upon participation and power sharing. One staff member reflected:

> The way I see it is . . . GEP is like in any organization, there are specifically people who are in power, like coordinators, EDs, directors; and at the same time there is this feeling in GEP that the responsibility or power is shared. (Leslie, program coordinator, age twenty-seven)

In other words, the organizational hierarchy dictated who had power and how decisions were to be made. Yet, simultaneously, the organization worked to create a culture of power sharing based upon its culture of empowerment. Perhaps the best description of GEP's decision-making practice was "choice within constraints." For example, while the director of programs was given a set budget and a schedule of "must-do" annual events or curriculum topics, the what and how of the daily program were largely left to the program team's creativity. In this way, it was not a supervisor "telling you what to do" but someone asking you, "What are you going to do to accomplish our organizational and programmatic goals? And what progress have you made?" As a result, while some staff struggled with this combined sense of autonomy and accountability, others loved the creative freedom the work provided and the personal challenge it entailed. They drew upon their creativity, personal strengths, and networks and developed gardening, meditation, and puberty curricula, as well as plays on HIV and AIDS, all under the content area of reproductive health and wellness.

The girls also experienced the "choice within constraints" model during their daily interactions with GEP program coordinators. As noted previously, GEP structured its curriculum around the five content areas and key annual events. However, girls had a say in what they wanted to do for these events and also in their daily activities. In many ways, this represented the magic of GEP. There was not a standardized curriculum or, rather, the standard curriculum was the women and the girls drawing upon their internal strengths and selves. They were the program's daily text. Thus, on one level, the possibilities were endless. On the other, budget, time, and programmatic commitments made to funding organizations were real limitations. This "choice within constraints" model drew upon the organization's culture of empowerment and represented how collective practices and personal power were manifested within the organizational hierarchy. In this way, GEP provided Black women and girls with the experiences of both being in positions of authority and sharing power.

Negotiating the competing decision-making strategies and their inherent understanding of power, however, was a challenge within GEP. For example, in regard to GEP's decision-making and power relations, Leslie also noted this:

> I think that is what GEP wants to do [share power], but I don't think that happens all the time. I think that with the new staff there are definitely some of us who acknowledge that it's OK to take some of this power, but there are definitely some gray areas where I've made a decision about such and such and, "Oh, you can't make that decision." And then it's like, "I thought I had this realm of power." "Well, you do, but that's not a part of that." And then it's like, "Whoa, I don't want to overstep those boundaries again, so maybe I need to back off." So I think I see some of that happening. And then there were times when you go to someone else to make the decision with the power and then it's like, "That's your decision," and they say, "Yeah, it is," so there's some unclarity about where one person ends and the other begins. (program coordinator, age twenty-seven)

The decision-making structure, and consequently the power structure within GEP, was oftentimes ambiguous due to lack of clarity regarding where one person's responsibilities or power ended and the other person's power began. Moreover, the criterion used to make individual and collective decisions was not clearly articulated within the organization. Thus staff experienced power as constantly negotiated, oftentimes contentious, and with the chance of punitive results.

This ambiguity existed at all levels and was often manifested in repeated calls for better communication. Throughout the research period, board members wanted a "more effective communication system with the E.D." and "more knowledge regarding the program" so they could "determine ways in which they could contribute more directly and effectively" (Gamble and Associates 1999, 5). In addition, GEP staff and the administrative team fell into phases of intense conflict over communication styles and communication systems. According to a program evaluator, "This was an area of considerable concern for staff. Some staff expressed frustration with the communication styles of program management, and perceived an environment in which they did not feel fully supported" (Gamble and Associates 1999, 3).

For example, during the final dress rehearsal for GEP's five-year anniversary event, the following occurred: As girls and program staff were walking through the program's schedule, a GEP board member arrived to assist with the process. Upon pulling out her program, staff realized that hers differed from the one they were using. The board member assured the staff that hers was the final version. The staff members copied and distributed this "finalized version" to rehearse with the girls. Girls learned their entrance and exit cues based upon this document. On the day of the event, however, something was wrong. The girls, program staff, and executive director were confused. The executive director wanted to know why the girls were not ready. The program director showed the executive director her program. Upon seeing the schedule used by the program team, the executive director was furious. "This is not the program that I gave you," she said. Bewildered, the program team responded, "But this is what the board member told us was the final version." The organization struggled through the event, and the incident was contentiously processed upon return. All participants wanted clearer, better communication. While the incident was clearly a case of miscommunication, during the process session that followed it was interpreted as a lack of respect for organizational power dynamics. In this case, the executive director argued that her power had been trivialized. With this assertion, the program team argued for clearer understanding and communication of the power dynamics, especially in relationship to decision making. During this research, two more contentious process retreats occurred during which GEP women discussed and confronted the issues over communications styles and lack of communication systems. As illustrated in the anniversary example, at the core of these disputes was the lack of clarity about power and authority.

In response to this "lack of clarity," some staff called for clear hierarchical power relations. As the executive director, Ife, noted:

> I've had the response that it's not traditional enough or male enough. I don't want to do it like that. It doesn't feel comfortable for me to do it like that. That's not who I am. "No, you got to do that. You have to just say what you want. We can't have a dialogue or be collective about it." That type of leadership, "Just tell me what to do," got projected a lot on me. The beauty for me was that I feel like I fought up against that—that I pushed people to maybe be in that whole collective mind-set. (age thirty-six)

This request is not unusual within women's organizations. Morken and Selle (1994) found that many women working in alternative women's organizations preferred formalized power to informal power structures (142). That is, contrary to some feminist assertions, collective decision making, especially consensus, can create opportunities for marginalization and silencing. They found that within some collectivist organizations, experienced activists with more resources could dominate the consensus process, and that bureaucracy offered a way to minimize this power and allow for more voices to be heard (142).

Morgen (1994) also found that the existence of an organizational "hierarchy could also serve as a 'protective shield' reducing the personal involvement in sensitive issues" (as quoted in Alvesson and Billing 1997, 116). In other words, GEP women were highly committed to the organization and to working with African American girls. Their work with GEP represented "opportunities for them to give something back and to do positive and powerful work with young Black women" (Gamble and Associates 1999, 16). Thus they were highly invested in their work as well as with the women and girls who made up this organizational world. Their requests for organizational hierarchy were ones for clarity regarding power relations as well as for the emotional and interpersonal distance that bureaucracy could provide in negotiating difficult decisions when there was a deep emotional investment.

This lack of clarity of how power should be and was moving within GEP also addressed women's lack of experience being in positions of formal power not only within GEP but in organizations in general. Danielle made the following remark:

> I think historically we are in a major shift in terms of women's power, because in some ways we are able to do things we weren't able to do before, and these organizations are coughing up these ideal models, but we still don't really have that many role models and resources to draw from; and we are also as women being asked to do everything we used to do plus all that, so it's overwhelming. I think people were scared to tap that power, and that creates a lot of messy, chaotic stuff that is hard to get through. (program coordinator, age twenty-six)

Danielle interpreted the "messy and chaotic" nature of power within GEP as manifestations of historical shifts in women's power and women's fear of their new power. This lack of organizational experience of being in power, let alone sharing power, was important. GEP was a young organization. By young, I am referring to the staff's biological age and work/supervisory experience. By all accounts, for the majority of GEP's program coordinators this was their first salaried job with benefits. Most had held hourly youth worker or retail positions prior to their tenure at GEP. In addition, the management team was composed of many first-time supervisors and board members.

Recognizing the lack of experience, GEP provided leadership training for all of its new staff members. "Facilitative Leadership" was an intensive four-day training program designed to help participants "contribute ideas and expertise, speak up when they have problems, take initiative, make decisions, and share responsibility for success" (Interaction Associates 1997, sect. 1-3). While elements of the training survived in the organization, it seemed difficult to incorporate the mood or spirit of the training into GEP's daily practice. Perhaps it was the harsh realities of Sun Valley, the lack of time, or the chaotic world of nonprofit service organizations, where "crises" dictated the flow and thus the spirit and dynamics within the agency. The fear of power; the lack of role models, especially organizational role models; and the lack of experience being in powerful organizational positions made it difficult for GEP's leadership to articulate, let alone develop, an effective model for integrating both hierarchical and shared power. In the end, two competing decision-making strategies containing conflicting definitions of power coexisted within the program. These two competing impulses structured organizational power relationships and practices. Both GEP staff and girls resisted what they interpreted as illegitimate power within the organization.

"THIS IS NOT IBM, IT IS A SISTERHOOD, RIGHT?"

As noted in the previous chapter, a key example of GEP women exercising power was the revision of the mission statement. With the shift from "The Urban Girl" to "The Strong Girl," GEP women redefined the organization, the girls, and, ultimately, themselves. It was an assertion of Black girlhood and womanhood that flew in the face of dominant representations of Black femaleness and contradicted organizational research suggesting that due to efforts to secure funding, nonprofits' mission statements often become more conservative over time (Helfgot [1974]1981; DiMaggio and Powell [1991] 1983). That is, despite its limitations, in the institutional world of nonprofits, asserting an Africentric womanist organizational identity was an assertion of power.

Moreover, GEP's Africentric womanist discourse fostered feelings of sisterhood within GEP. Both GEP's board of directors and staff members, most of whom were Black women, had come into the organization not only because they wanted to work with Black girls but also for the opportunity to work with other Black women and to be valued as a Black woman. One staff member noted:

> Coming here was a huge decision and I felt like equally I could give, but the benefits I could reap would be amazing, and would be just as much as I could give . . . I was inspired to check it out . . . part of it is definitely the staff, sisters, being women, and I think who could better inspire and help motivate and show young women what it means to be a woman than other women who look and share those experiences they had. I thought one would be to build relationships with other like-minded women who were interested in working with girls, so just in terms of networking that would be positive and

in terms of friendships. Also in terms of what I get—I think that in a lot of other jobs that I have been with it has just been my skills and the things that I have gained through schooling and education, but not necessarily my experiences as a woman have not been valued or taken into account or even thought of . . . but this is a time when I am looked at as a whole person. (Cheryl, program coordinator age twenty-five)

Cheryl's expectations of being seen as a "whole person," being valued as a Black woman, and developing and sharing a special bond with other Black women were shared by many GEP staff members as well as board members.

In addition, staff members described feeling, for the first time, empowered as Black women as a result of working at GEP. Leslie reflected:

There was *not* a deep historical knowledge about who I was as a Black woman—African woman. I have always felt that something was missing, and this led me down a particular path that I didn't have to go. One of the best strengths about GEP is that it teaches Black girls who they are . . . I am learning who I am. (program coordinator, age twenty-seven)

Similarly, Kailana noted:

I think I have grown. I think I've been doing an inner search thing since I've started working here because I'm working with Black women. I'm learning like the girls. . . . Oh God, it's so big for me, you just don't know, sometimes I just cry about it. . . . I'm understanding that, I'm OK. (program coordinator, age twenty-four)

For Kailana and Leslie, working at GEP was an empowering period of self-growth and learning. They and many of their colleagues were still in the process of developing the sense of self and strategies they were hired to teach the girls. In this way, the organization became a safe space or homeplace for the staff. Staff members, in particular, did not want to work for an "IBM," where it was assumed that they might have to leave their Black womanness at the door or risk not being treated with respect. They also viewed "IBM" as having limited the opportunities for Black women to exercise power and develop strong and positive relationships with other Black women. They came to GEP to be part of a sisterhood.

"Sisterhood," however, was fraught with tension. One board member reflected:

. . . [when] I think of sisterhood I look at being a Delta,[4] with my own relationship with my sister, and it isn't always pleasant, and it's so familiar and comfortable. . . . But sometimes the business doesn't get done and we need to call people out and sisterhood is sometimes about telling people they aren't doing their job. It's not always flowers, "coochie-coo." There will be jealousy and different things. People think sisterhood is a perfect state, and people try to get along the best they can. Because we are all women or Black women or whatever, you would think we would have a better relationship or a better way to get along, but sometimes we do and sometime we don't. (Karen, board member, age forty-five)

Though they recognized the conflict between the expectations and realities of sisterhood, Karen and her GEP "sisters" still expected the negatives to be kept at bay.

During moments of conflict, GEP women often drew upon the discourse of sisterhood as a strategy to shape intra-organizational power dynamics. One particular situation brought to a head the issue of sisterhood: a pregnant staff member. Maya was the coordinator for group B, girls ranging from ages eleven to fourteen. Maya was twenty-three years old, not married, and in the process of completing her bachelor's degree. Her pregnancy sparked controversy among the staff, girls, and community residents. Similar to the judgments resident staff members received, she was immediately judged an unsuitable role model for the girls—a criticism the girls also levied against her. For instance, at her baby shower, GEP girls—her girls—gave her condoms as a shower gift. It was a stinging critique.

Sending the organization into turmoil, however, were the conditions of Maya's maternity leave. At a weekly staff meeting, Yasmine, the coordinator for older girls, ages sixteen and up, asked about Maya's maternity leave. She had been hearing rumors and wanted to get "some clarity" about the issues. Specifically, Yasmine wanted to know if the organization had a maternity leave policy and if it was paid. The short answer was "no." To this, Aisha, the group A coordinator, and Yasmine remarked, "Well, what kind of sisterhood is this?"

The debate around the lack of paid maternity leave created such a controversy and generated so much tension that at the suggestion of outside evaluators the executive director hired an outside consultant to conduct a process retreat around the meaning of sisterhood in relation to the women's work at GEP. At the retreat, staff defined sisterhood in myriad ways: Sisterhood "is more personal than womanist," "It means you understand each other's pieces," "It's like family—for better or for worse, good and bad, you have to work it out—some days it might get ugly, but you are committed to working it out." The tension centered on the balance between "what is sisterhood and what is our professional standard." For program coordinators, sisterhood meant that they were "given time to explain why something didn't get done." In other words, "We get patience, but that doesn't mean we're allowed to slack." They also understood sisterhood as working in organizations with women-friendly work policies and an environment free from oppression and fear. Staff accused the organization of failing to live up to its mission, in hopes of shaping both personal and organizational practices. Staff, in this instance, employed sisterhood to "speak truth to power" within the organization. Administrators, on the other hand, felt that staff members were using sisterhood as a means of "shirking" responsibilities and forcing special privileges. In other words, the location of the women in the organizational hierarchy shaped and structured how they articulated and experienced sisterhood within the organization. Those subject to administrative power used sisterhood to challenge what they saw as unfair treatment. Those in power used sisterhood to demand higher standards of personal accountability.

One of the difficulties in analyzing resistance is that "resistance" is linked to multiple theoretical traditions and has been used to describe a variety of sometimes conflicting social actions.[5] Resistance can be hidden or direct, thick or thin, oppositional or accommodating. Moreover, resistance does not guarantee social change. For example, due to our multiple positioning, resistance in one area can often lead to a reproduction of oppression along other axes (Crenshaw 1992; Cohen 1999; Craig 2002). In addition, resistance, especially thin oppositions, often located on the cultural level in the realm of everyday practices, can be partial and lead to an unintended reproduction of power relations (Willis 1977; hooks and West 1992). Despite these uneven (and at times reproductive) outcomes, understanding how and under what conditions people resist is important for understanding strategies of how power moves within an organization.

"DOING POWER" GEP GIRL STYLE

GEP staff members were not the only ones who resisted organizational practices and authority. To the staff's frustration, GEP girls often used their feet and their voices to challenge the staff's generational and organizational power. Thus, contrary to the macro-structural and the organizational hierarchy that located poor Black girls at the bottom of the power ladder, GEP girls walked in and walked out of the program as well as talked back to GEP staff and larger institutional forces.

Walking in, Walking out

First and foremost, GEP girls walked into the program. Roxanne, GEP's administrative director, noted: "I think a lot of the reasons the girls are in GEP is because the girls push for it; I don't think it's a buy-in by the parents so much as it's a buy-in by the girls." Girls echoed this sentiment. Remembering her first day at GEP, Alisha reflected:

> I asked her [my cousin] where everybody was at and she said at GEP. She walked me up here and I went to the door. . . . So [the next day] I went back and I had my homework. I did my homework. Then I just started coming back and telling my grandpa to drop me off. (GEP girl, age thirteen)

Similarly, Diamond remembered:

> When I was little I came to GEP. And I used to leave because I hated it, then I went back to Mansell [a different after-school program], then back to GEP. (GEP girl, age twelve)

Girls attended GEP because *they* wanted to. Within Sun Valley there were four additional free after-school programs that GEP girls could attend. In other words, while girls might not have had a choice about attending an after-school program, they often did have a choice about which one to attend. Walking in provided GEP girls an opportunity to exert some power over their lives.

For grant-dependent, non-profit organizations, client contact hours, or youth attendance, is critical. Unlike schools and juvenile justice agencies, which can enforce student participation and attendance with the support of state-sanctioned policies and police, the staff at GEP had to rely upon the genuine interest of the young women, personal connections, and various and sundry perks to keep girls coming back to the program. One key perk was a small stipend girls received for attending the program. The stipend was a financial learning tool rather than a direct payment for attendance, and the actual amounts of the stipend varied by age group, ranging from five to ten dollars a month. As part of the financial curriculum, girls were required to place their checks within a savings account. GEP staff kept the savings books, and girls had to submit a written withdrawal request to remove funds. While girls often looked forward to "bank day," this small financial incentive did not impact their participation. In other words, their attendance and participation were always optional.

During my tenure at GEP, enrollment was a standing item on the staff meeting agenda. This was a particularly tense topic for the program coordinators who worked with the older girls, ages sixteen and up. During my first staff meeting, Yasmine, the program coordinator for the older girls, was asked to present her recruitment plan. After her presentation, the executive director challenged her strategies and reminded her that "if she could not bring in more girls, we will lose the funding for her position." After the meeting, Yasmine approached me almost in tears, asking, "Do you have any ideas on how to get more girls into the program?" At that moment I realized that the girls were not at the bottom of the organizational hierarchy. Though at the outset the young women might be indebted to GEP for its services, at a particular point, this dependency was transferred, and GEP staff became indebted to the young women for continued funding and, ultimately, employment. Instead of being passive recipients of GEP's services, girls simultaneously redefined themselves and were redefined by staff as consumers with the power to take their business elsewhere. As Diamond noted earlier, she often went back and forth between the local after-school programs. In her words, "I used to leave because I hated it." Similarly, Tangee recalled: "The reason why I stopped coming is cause, it started to get boring, and I was like, 'Uhh uhh.' " While small in scope and individual in nature, taking up the position of a consumer and walking out was a form of power that created a pathway for girls to resist GEP staff and programming. Moreover, this form of resistance held little risk for GEP girls. It was indirect, and the confrontations or challenges with the staff were little to nonexistent. Also, if or when the girls returned to the organization, the staff welcomed them back.

While walking in was important, walking out represented a stronger assertion of girls' power. Although one might argue that walking out signals powerlessness or disengagement, one particular incident shifted my interpretation of this strategy. Alisha recounted:

> When Denise first came . . . they was like, "This is y'alls new coordinator" and stuff like that. And then we were in the room sitting down and Denise came and she was like, she just met us and she said hi to us in a nice way and then she just screamed at us—telling us what we should do and shouldn't do, just that same minute she just came. And then I guess people left. . . . We were all like, "Denise is doing too much, we don't want her to be our coordinator." (GEP girl, age eleven)

In this moment, many girls, unhappy with the new program coordinator "screaming at them, telling what they should do," left. They simply packed up early and went home. This collective leaving, as the phrase "we were all like" implies, had a profound effect on the new staff member. She had to reevaluate and quickly rework her relationship strategies and, more important, her own power with the girls. That day, she lost "numbers," and failure to maintain or grow her enrollments immediately jeopardized her job and perhaps current and future funding of the organization. She had to learn how power really moved within GEP. Unlike walking in, which spoke to girls' power as consumers, walking out represented a more collective resistance and highlighted the girls' push for partnership within GEP. In the preceding example, walking out was not about taking their business else-where; instead, it was about changing the terms of engagement within the organization. They did not want her to be their coordinator! Walking out was a strategy that girls used to shape the organization and the program to fit their needs.

Talking Back

Girls also talked back to challenge the staff's generational and organizational power. According to hooks (1989), "talking back" is "speaking to an author-ity figure, as if they were equals" (5). It represents a refusal to be subordinate, to be silent, to be invisible, and is therefore a negation of dominant ideolo-gies and practices compelling the marginalized to silence, obedience, and passivity. Best (2000), drawing upon hooks, locates this resistance practice "with the play between power and opposition to power recognizing both con-trol and defiance. Young people talk back to challenge . . . those who control them—adults" (146).

One powerful example of girls "talkin' back" was the Nia Collective's community block party. The Nia Collective, which draws its name from the Kiswahili word for "purpose," was a leadership program within the organization composed of 13–16-year-old girls. Tangee (age sixteen) responded that her favorite part of GEP was Nia, because "when we do like a project for Nia we get to do the project by ourselves, like we the staff . . . like Ife and them had no say so." Similarly, Alisha (age thirteen) noted: "When we do projects for Nia, we're in charge." As part of the Nia Collec-tive, girls explicitly explored issues of race, class, and gender as well as notions of giving back and activism. They also examined how these sys-tems played out in their everyday lives at home, at school, and in the larger Bay City community.

As noted in the opening of this book, during the community block party there was a conflict over what the adults perceived as sexualized dancing of some of the talent show participants. According to the girls, the executive director was mad and wanted to know "who let those girls go up on stage and dance like that." Kisha, one of the Nia Collective emcees for the event, reminded Ife: "You do get your opinion, but you can't do anything about it." Similarly, Tangee noted, "This was for us . . . you really don't have no say" (GEP girl, age sixteen). By refusing to be silent or invisible, Tangee and Kisha challenged the generational and organizational hierarchy and asserted their authority as youth and as "staff for the event." In other words, despite their subordinate placement within the organizational hierarchy and within larger generational systems of power, they openly resisted the executive director's attempt to silence their voices and challenge their power.

Reflecting on the event, Rolanda, also a Nia participant, proclaimed:

> The executive director had a funky attitude. It's not your thing! Did you help paint? Do your back hurt? Get your clothes dirty? I don't think so, so why you mad? WE should be the ones that's mad. So I said I wasn't taking the executive director's stuff, so I got up and left. Mostly everybody left. (GEP girl, age eleven)

Once again GEP girls collectively left what they understood to be an unfair situation. In her work on the politics of girls' anger, Brown (1998) writes that anger is threatening to those in power "not only because it might be followed by action, but also because it signals that subordinates take themselves seriously. They believe they have the capacity as well as the right to be the judges of those around them" (11). Girls' anger holds political potential because it identifies their "resistant knowing voices."

For most of the program coordinators, their jobs at GEP placed them in positions of generational and organizational authority for the first time. Monica, an eighteen-year-old intern in the program, summed up her and many of her colleagues' experiences on authority and relationship building with girls. She noted, "It was a mixture, easy to work with girls because they can relate to me, but then at the same time hard because I am so young." Due to their youth as well as their inexperience being in positions of authority, it was often a challenge for many of the programs coordinators to recognize and access their own power inside an outside of the organization. As a result, girls' assertion of power was not read or experienced as "girl power" or empowerment but, rather, as moments of disrespect or disregard for the staff's authority. In the talent show example, the executive director, frustrated with the girls' back talk, attempted to strip the girls of their voice. In other words, despite the organizational mission, individual staff often intentionally and unintentionally sought to maintain their organizational and generational power. Nonetheless, even with such knee-jerk reactions from individual staff members, GEP's organizational space was one wherein girls' back talk was

protected. So how can we explain this open and direct challenge to generational and organizational authority?

GEP'S ORGANIZATIONAL POWER MATRIX

An organization's power matrix addresses the state of play of power relationships within an organizational space and is built upon the organization's
environment, culture, and structure. These organizational features serve as
domains of power that intersect and interact, often in contradictory and
competing ways, oftentimes disrupting macro-structural power relations. In
this case, the organizational power matrix determined the resources that
GEP's women and girls mobilized to imagine, articulate, and negotiate power.
That is, while poor Black girls are theorized to exist at the bottom of race,
class, gender, and age hierarchies, this was not the case within GEP. Within
this space, Black women and girls were not marginal but were centered, and
this position of being centered in and of itself provided a base of power, often
understood as support, that was critical to the girls' identity work.

Specifically, GEP's Africentric womanist and youth development discourses created frames that not only challenged dominant ideologies regarding girls' silence, passivity, and submissiveness but also provided GEP girls
with discourses that supported their power. Similar to the ways that African
Americans and women used the U.S. Constitution, GEP girls drew upon
these discourses to push the organization to live up to its own goal of
"enabling Black girls." In addition, GEP's non-profit status created an opportunity for the girls to shift their organizational positioning from clients to
consumers and, at times, partners. These frames, as well as the girls' shifting
location as consumers and partners, were mobilized during such conflicts via
group. As noted earlier, group was a critical part of GEP's daily curriculum. It
was also the designated space where conflicts were resolved. According to
Ananda, group was a space

> where we can get to the dirty stuff. You know what I mean? A forum
> for us as women and for girls where we're able to just be safe. And
> that's hard, that's really hard because . . . we've lost those, those
> places. (dance instructor, age thirty-five)

Group was the space in GEP where safety and respect were nurtured and
individual and collective violations discussed. Thus in addition to the weekly
curriculum, group was put into action such that each major conflict, or time
that the girls collectively talked back to and/or walked out of the program,

was just the beginning of the story. For example, almost immediately after the talent show, the girls and staff held a group session. Tangee remembered: "Yeah, after everything we sat in a little circle and talked about it. We said somethin' and the staff got to talk." Leslie, a GEP program coordinator, shared that "during group we expressed our concerns about the dancing. We tried to explain that the way those young girls were moving their bodies made them targets, made them sex objects, and that had an impact on their reputations, their safety." Rolanda told the staff that "they needed to get with it because this is what girls, what youth, were doing." Girls also expressed their frustration at not being able to "be the staff" as promised. In the end, the girls' "back talk" did not result in a ban from the program or in any restrictions from participating in the future activities. In fact, no privileges were lost. Instead, and most importantly, both the women and girls stayed connected to each other and the program.

Group created a space of change within the organization that not only made it safer to walk out and talk back but also made walking out and talking back viable strategies. For example, in a letter to program supporters and the board of directors, the cofounder of GEP noted this:

> Problems? Sure! Our older girls are very resistant to GEP's structure . . . they are simply not very receptive to what we're offering. So we're attempting to meet this challenge through greater flexibility, innovative program ideas, and more individual contact. (GEP, 1998, 2)

Two points about girls' resistance are highlighted in this correspondence. First, staff recognized girls as "resistant to GEP's structure and offerings" and, second, this resistance resulted in GEP staff "meeting the challenge" by altering relationships and program content. Group was the space where these "challenges were met" and changes in the program conceived and put into practice. Thus talking back and walking out were forms of direct resistance tied to features of GEP's organizational context. Girls can talk back and walk out of a variety of settings. However, in many contexts, talking back or walking out are ineffectual strategies that often distance girls from adult-run institutions. GEP's organizational ethos and practices responded to the girls in ways that made talking back and walking out moves within a conversation. While individual staff may have reacted to girls' defiance by attempting to silence or control the girls, the organization's practice was to bring the girls back into the dialogue. Through group, girls became organizational partners rather than clients or consumers. Yet group alone cannot transform the public sphere. To create social change, GEP women and girls must move outside of this fragile and tenuous space to challenge larger structures of domination.

PROTESTING POWER

In her work on girls' c/overt resistance and the role of girlzines, Schilt (2003) suggests that zines provide a social space within which girls can develop a critical consciousness necessary for both individual and collective resistance. GEP appeared to be such a space. For example, Nyema reported this:

> I talk to people about being a Black woman. I find myself doing it unconsciously. And sometimes they don't want to hear that . . . I find myself saying, "Don't say that word around me" Shut up, the B word and the N word, three words that I just cannot tolerate, especially directed at me, and I stand up for that. (GEP girl and intern, age seventeen)

While girls relayed many examples of "standing up for themselves" and talking back outside of GEP, I was also fortunate to witness an example of girls "taking it to the streets". In 2000, GEP girls organized against Proposition 21, the California "Gang Violence and Juvenile Crime Prevention" initiative. This initiative was a vicious attack on youth, especially poor youth of color, which authorized placing youth as young as age fourteen into the adult "justice" system and adult jails. It also reduced confidentiality protections for youth offenders. GEP girls spoke out against the initiative. For example, Tangee (age sixteen) wrote:

> My Feelings about Prop 21
>
> If Prop 21 passes, I would be scared of the police around me,
> the guns they carry, the bars I'd be behind. . . .
> If Prop 21 passes, young youth that stand on the corner
> with the same color on is going to get picked up by the police.
> If Prop 21 passes, young youth would not have freedom.
> So if you feel like me, and you love your kids
> Please VOTE NO ON PROP 21.

The girls did not stop with words. As part of their protest against Proposition 21, GEP girls engaged in door-to-door outreach, participated in city-wide youth demonstrations, teach-ins, and rallies, and hosted a community town hall forum on the issue. As part of their community forum, they read their poetry and shared facts about the proposition in an effort to engage, educate, and encourage eligible community members to vote against it. Finally, in perhaps the most "traditional" form of open resistance, GEP girls took to the streets with other youth and protested in front of city hall. In her description of enabling, Ife, the executive director, noted:

> We never set the political action agenda for girls. We could have empowered them to set up campaigns about violence in their community, [but] instead we were hoping for some inspiration from them. . . . I think if we were empowering them, we might have set the agenda and then let them carry the picket signs. (age thirty-six)

GEP staff did not set the agenda for girls' political engagement. According to Monica, GEP intern and Nia coordinator, GEP girls "really educated themselves about the proposition." Armed with this information, they met with other youth groups and brainstormed potential strategies and tactics. Again, Nia Collective participants were the "staff for these events." Their interests, initiative, and commitment drove this protest. In sum, girls took the skills learned within GEP and in relationship with GEP staff and applied these strategies to challenge larger systems of inequality that reproduced their race, class, and generational subordination. Despite the passage of the proposition, the young women very openly and directly resisted their generational and class subordination and acquired valuable lessons about power and empowerment. While one example may not be enough to suggest consistent practice and long-term empowerment, it does provide a glimpse into the possibilities that GEP offered its participants. GEP girls developed an emergent culture of resistance that moved beyond the organization's borders.

In sum, within GEP, some everyday social relations were disrupted with the effect of creating a space in which Black girls were able to resist their generational and organizational subordination. Consequently, power moved through GEP in ways and with results that the founders and even staff did not anticipate. GEP's organizational context mediated and reshaped the power relations between the women and the girls and ultimately created a space for the girls to resist their subordination. GEP girls were able to talk back, and GEP staff listened to what they had to say. This altered access to power has implications for the negotiation of Black womanhood within GEP. The negotiation and representation of Black womanhood is the subject of chapters 5 and 6.

5

Africentric Womanist Femininity
Meets Decent Girl Femininity

That makes me think about what femininity is, like how it is a spectrum and you can define what it is for yourself and it doesn't have to
be one extreme or the other. (Cheryl, program coordinator, age
twenty-five)

So here we are with our standards, but whose standards are we presenting to the girls, whose standards are we telling the girls are OK?
(Roxanne, administrative director, age fifty-four)

Femininities are social scripts that contain abstract ideals for what members
of the category of woman are and should be. They are culturally and socially
appropriate road maps for "what to do" and "how to be" a woman (Schippers
2004). While all forms of femininity are constructed in the context of the
overall subordination of women to men, they are also constructed in relation
to other femininities (Connell 1987). In other words, Black women's reality
is much more complicated than

> one of an external white society objectifying black women as the
> Other with a unified Black community staunchly challenging these
> external assaults. Instead, Black women find themselves in a web of
> cross-cutting relationships, each presenting varying combinations of
> images and Black women's self definitions. (Collins 1991, 96)

In this chapter, I explore GEP staff's Africentric womanist femininity and GEP girls' decent girl femininity. Specifically, drawing upon their Africentric womanist ideology, GEP women identified self-definition, self-determination, and sexual agency as three key qualities of an Africentric womanist femininity. This femininity became the staff's "standard" and, as a result, alternative Black femininities were marginalized within the organization. Yet GEP girls were not empty vessels waiting to be filled with the Africentric womanist cup. They brought their own nascent decent girl Black femininity into the program. Their femininity, grounded in the realities of Sun Valley, also emphasized self-definition, self-determination, and sexual agency, however, aspects of the girls' "how to be" and "what to do" regarding Black femininity differed from that put forth by the staff.

AFRICENTRIC WOMANIST FEMININITY

For GEP women, Africentric womanist femininity represented an oppositional identity that could support Black women's and girls' internal validation as well as external success. For GEP staff, strong girls and powerful women were those who were able to self-define, self-determine, and act as agents of their own sexuality.

Self-Definition

GEP staff understood self-definition as the ability to define who you are on your own terms. This was a critical component of Africentric womanist femininity. Ife noted that "a strong sense of self" was one of the biggest challenges facing young Black girls. She stated:

> It's a challenge, and I don't know if I can articulate it, because I know I'm really scared and feeling unknowledgeable about it, but I think that if females don't have a strong identity and a strong sense of self, there are some external factors that are going to do a lot of defining for us. (executive director, age thirty-six)

Collins (1991) argues that self-definition is a "preoccupation" of Black women that underscores their struggle to "reconcile the contradictions separating [their] internally defined images of self as African American women with [their] objectification as the Other" (94). GEP staff echoed this concern. Self-definition was considered critical to Black women's and girls' health, sanity, and survival. For example, in response to the question "What is a healthy or successful Black woman?" Asha remarked:

> You no longer perceive yourself on how the outside world perceives you . . . you self-define yourself, and there is a big honoring inside of you. (program coordinator, age twenty-six)

Similarly, Cheryl noted:

> When I was growing up messages were just like, "You are supposed to"—all that stuff about the good girl box, the values you are supposed to have. You are supposed to be intelligent, but not outshine guys, not have your intelligence be a threat to males. You are supposed to be beautiful and well kept—do the whole makeup thing, but not that sexy where you are attracting all this attention on you. . . . It's not even a myth about the Black woman having to be strong and stuff because that is what we had to do in our experience here but that shouldn't be, the vision shouldn't be limited to just that. . . . What a young woman is shouldn't have to be defined by other people, she should leave that open. . . . I think it has to do with women being able to define themselves without looking to other people to be affirmed—knowing that you "have it going on." You just know, you are affirmed within yourself. (program coordinator, age twenty-five)

As Cheryl noted, Black girls must navigate hegemonic constructions of White femininity, hypersexualized representations of Black femininity, and the Strong Black Woman.

The Strong Black Woman, or "SBW," as cultural critic Joan Morgan (1999) calls her, is a representation of Black womanhood celebrated by both dominant and indigenous groups that is often viewed as "a more empowering alternative to the dominant construction of white womanhood" (Beauboeuf-Lafontant 2005, 106). She is imagined as one who can bear everything and still stand as the backbone of her family. She can "tolerate the intolerable" (106). While the intent may have been to celebrate Black women's survival against what are often insurmountable odds, this femininity is also limited. The SBW supports the false assumption that Black women do not need to be empowered—that they have achieved equality and justice. Moreover, this "strength training . . . leaves little room for girls and subsequently women to acknowledge their full humanity" and "renders self-concern literally inconceivable" (112, 119). It is with and against these representations of Black femininity that GEP women and girls attempt to forge self-identities. Cheryl wanted girls to be able to resist both dominant and indigenous representa-tions of Black femininity. Self-definition involved stepping outside of such "external valuations" and rejecting these controlling images (Collins 1991).

GEP women identified constructing a strong racialized gender identity as the first part of the self-definition process. In order to accomplish this task, Black women and girls must first revisit and rethink what they have been taught about their history. Ananda noted:

> Another thing about a healthy Black woman is that we understand where we came from. And that doesn't mean that we know what it is to be in Africa or African, because we're not anymore. It's African American. You know? Unless—your parents were born on the con-tinent or you were born there—and immigrated or whatever, you are no longer African by experience. You are African American. And really being able to embrace that, you know . . . and how we've sustained ourselves here. And that that is our first glory. There's a beauty about, you know, growing up here and having the stories that came directly from our lines, as opposed to only validating what came from this other place that we're no longer connected to through experience. (dance instructor, age thirty-five)

Ananda connected Black women's identity with African American history and rewrote the story of slavery as a story of survival, as African Americans' "first glory." This revisionist history challenged traditional readings of the African American experience as well as strict African-centered renderings of the past. That is, instead of reading slave narratives as sources of defeat and shame, she suggested that African Americans are the ultimate survivors. Through the process of reclaiming and celebrating Black folks' survival sto-ries in the United States, GEP women and girls could construct a more accu-rate picture of their past that allowed them to understand and make connections to their present-day realities and representations.

Learning Black herstory also provided women and girls with models of how to survive. Aisha reflected:

> And as a Black woman, I think it's very necessary for a healthy Black woman to know a lot about her history. Because I think to know, of course, the old cliché, "To know where you come from is to know where you're going." I feel like that is so necessary for us to know because we've been through so much . . . it would help, it helps me, to keep going. Cuz like, "Oh, OK, I know I'm going through this right now but look what Fannie Lou Hammer went

through, look at Harriet Tubman, what did she use to get past this hump, because the hump I'm going through, boy I prefer this load than that load, you know, I prefer to learn from her load than to carry it." So I think it's so necessary to . . . know our Black herstory. (program coordinator, age twenty-three)

Black herstory provided Aisha with examples of Black "sheroes" surviving and thriving in what seemed to be impossible circumstances. Their stories helped her continue in spite of the very real barriers and obstacles she faced in her daily life. In this way, Black herstory provided models of how "to be" and "do" Black womanhood.

Coming to terms with Black herstory created an opportunity for women and girls to reject the controlling images of Black women in circulation in mainstream as well as indigenous communities. Studying the lives of Black women offered an occasion to admire and love Black women, to love, value, and respect oneself. Within GEP, staff understood self-love as a manifestation of self-definition and a requirement for self-determination. Ananda continued:

A healthy Black woman loves herself unconditionally. She knows she is where she's supposed to be. . . . She recognizes that she is a work in progress. Self-love has to do with everything that she is, both physically, spiritually, emotionally, and all that that contains. (dance instructor, age thirty-five)

Similarly, Maya noted:

It has just been bred into us not to really focus on ourselves, on our self-love, and I think it is really important to teach women that you need to nurture yourself and give self-love, because in order for you to really help anyone else you have to help yourself. (program coordinator, age twenty-three)

This "loving of self unconditionally" and "nurturing of self" spoke to GEP's womanist underpinnings and also addressed the difficulty of such love for Black women moving between and among racist and sexist representations and practices.

As a result, self-love came to be seen as political, as a statement against oppressive structures and degrading discourses. Danielle remarked:

I think that it is very political to be fostering self-love in young Black girls. I think it is more political than a lot of other things that are typically described as political. Because I think empowered Black girls will hopefully grow up to be empowered Black women, and that is awesome because it has the power to really change the world. To change communities, families—to let people know, to just give them more power as they walk the path of being a Black women, which means that if they are more powerful then they are hopefully going to demand that they have access to things and their rights are equal and hopefully they will pass it on and continue to empower people. I think that self-love is a movement that is often-times more powerful than registering people to vote in some ways. (program coordinator, age twenty-six)

Through redefining oneself, one could love that which was self, not the stereotyped representations of Black femaleness fed to Black women and girls. In this way, self-love came to represent a political process within GEP—one that could only be accomplished through knowledge of one's Black herstory and the process of self-definition. As bell hooks suggests:

Collectively, black people and our allies in struggle are empowered when we practice self-love as a revolutionary intervention that undermines practices of domination. Loving blackness as political resistance transforms our ways of looking and being, and thus cre-ates conditions necessary for us to move against the forces of domi-nation and death and reclaim black life. (1992, 20)

Loving Black womanness was at the center of GEP and its daily program. It was as if it were painted on the walls.

This ethos was so prevalent throughout the organization that the princi-pal investigator for a program evaluation of GEP noted the following:

The strength of the program is the racial/gender pride component. A clear indicator of this component's success (enrichment program) is demonstrated in the participants' responses to attaining self-esteem and racial and gender pride. When asked what they have learned from the program and what GEP is doing for African Amer-ican women, the groups yielded a myriad of answers, i.e., "Stop hating each other," "Get a good education," and "Don't get preg-nant," all of which showed their understanding that love of self is a love for one's race. (Clark and Associates 1996, 13)

I include this quote not because I agree with the investigator's interpretation of these comments as support for racial and gender pride but, rather, to illustrate that GEP's identity work was easily recognizable by those inside and outside of the organization. Nyema, a GEP girl and intern, noted:

> I don't see how anybody can go out of GEP and truly be like labeled or called a successful GEP girl and have a negative view of other black women—I mean of course there are people who are just bad people, but just a general stereotypical negative view, portraying a negative view of women, uh uh, we don't do that. Disrespecting ourselves? We don't do that. (age seventeen)

GEP's racial and gender pride component, its promotion of self-definition and self-love, was the foundation of the organization's identity·work.

Self-Determination

Self-determination, or the power to decide one's own destiny, was the second core theme of GEP's Africentric womanist femininity. GEP staff had a multivalent understanding of self-determination. On the one hand, staff understood it to mean being financially independent. On the other hand, self-determination also spoke to psychological and emotional independence that allowed young women to stand strong in their beliefs and make decisions that were best for them. For example, in response to "What are the qualities of a successful GEP girl?," Maya reflected:

> What would be a successful GEP girl? Someone who can critically think out situations. Being able to analyze situations and know what's right and what's wrong for yourself. Because what's right for you may not necessarily be right for somebody else. So showing some independence away from family, especially if you do come from a destructive family environment. To be able to step away from that and say, "You know what, the situation that I'm in is a little screwed up and some of the people that I am around are a little screwed up, too, but I'm not gonna own that and I'm not gonna make it feel like it's something that I have to carry on. So I want to see something different for myself." So being able to make some positive choices and some positive goals and trying to do what they need to do to reach it. And just wanting to be some—show some type of leadership skills, even if it is redirecting themselves from that family pattern or going to college or deciding that they don't want to go to college and that they want to work. (program coordinator, age twenty-three)

Maya constructed self-determination as psychological and intellectual independence, as the ability to critically think or challenge both dominant and indigenous expectations, relationships, and ideologies. It was the ability to withstand peer pressure and to "show some leadership" or not to follow the crowd's beliefs or practices. This independence in thought was considered important for all Black females, but especially important for GEP girls, who potentially had "destructive family environments" and oftentimes more opportunities to make decisions that could negatively impact their future.

Yasmine agreed. She reflected:

> I think the main thing that I like to see is a girl start to think for herself and be comfortable being, if necessary, independent in her thought. You know, as far as being comfortable saying to her friends, the peer group, "Uh, you know I gotta go to class, I can't be cutting because I'm having a test next week." I mean, even if it's something as small as that, giving them the power within themselves to say, "This is what I want to do, I don't want to be a failure, I want to do something with my life, more than what I see around me. I think that any girl that I work with I try to instill that, speak up for yourself and use your power." (program coordinator, age thirty)

Within GEP's Africentric womanist femininity, Black women and girls were encouraged to look to one's self rather than relying on others, especially their peers, for leadership. Girls were also encouraged to see and acknowledge their own power. Often using the language of voice, staff encouraged the girls to "use their power and speak up for themselves."

GEP staff also urged girls to be economically self-sufficient ". . . you know, show some type of independence, some type of taking care of themselves" (Maya, program coordinator, age twenty-three). Other GEP staff agreed. Yasmine stated:

> I think that the message does come across clearly to them that the only thing we expect from them is for them to be able to be independent and live their lives, to live and not have the government live their lives for them. (program coordinator, age thirty)

Yasmine articulated an ethos of self-determination that rejected Black women's dependency on the state for survival. She understood welfare dependency and "being caught up" in the criminal justice system as having "the government live" your life and as a condition of dependence, a place of vulnerability and lack of freedom.

Staff also interpreted dependency on men as being equally detrimental to a young woman's self-determination. Cheryl related:

I was given those messages about Black women as being independent and self-sufficient, and I had it in me to be a mother if need be, by myself . . . you don't really need a man. (program coordinator, age twenty-five)

Aisha asserted:

You can't depend so much on that man. I think it's unhealthy to depend solely on that person and not depend on yourself. . . . That if something happened—if you got divorced, you left him, he left you, he died—that you could still make it in your life without falling apart spiritually, financially, and physically. You know what I'm saying. And that's specific to being a woman. (program coordinator, age twenty-three)

Yasmine stressed:

I think we're definitely taught as women, we're absolutely positively taught as women that we need a man in order to be a complete person. It's in everything, everything that we do. . . . When we talk about the fact that I'm thirty years old and I'm not married and I don't have a kid, and women, older women in my family are saying, "When you gettin' married?" Or, "When you gonna' have a kid?" And it's like, "Well, what's wrong with me now?" It's like we're taught something is wrong with us if we don't have a husband, or young girls have to lie about having a boyfriend, "Oh, I got a boyfriend," when they really don't. The message their getting is it's not OK if they don't. So definitely teaching them that it's OK to be independent women, it's OK not to need anything from a pimp, or it's OK to be self-sufficient. (program coordinator, age thirty)

Staff understood that girls received mixed messages regarding men. On the one hand, girls were taught that men completed them. On the other hand, Black girls were constantly prepared to be independent and self-sufficient women who did not depend upon or need a man to be somebody. GEP emphasized the latter position, and, consequently, economic self-sufficiency was understood within the organization as one of the critical steps toward self-determination. Much of the program's curriculum focused on preparing the young women to live self-sufficient lives. Economic development, aca-demic enrichment, gender and ethnic pride, reproductive health (pregnancy prevention), and leadership, all of the program's core curriculum areas, sought to provide the young women with opportunities to develop their tal-ents, to learn skills, to increase their educational outcomes, and to acquire needed information to put them on the path of social mobility. Here, if a young woman could think outside of dominant and indigenous stereotypes, resist peer and family pressure, and use her voice, then she would have the internal tools necessary to recover and rediscover herself—to self-determine. The final step toward self-determination was sexual agency.

Sexual Agency

Not surprisingly, anxiety about sex and representations of Black women's sexuality loomed large in the narratives shared by the women I interviewed. Women viewed this emphasis on sex as new—specific to this generation of girls raised on rap music and MTV. For example, Maya, a twenty-three-year-old college student raised in a small Northern California community, reflected:

> I think when I grew up, I was still playing with Barbie dolls until I was like ten or eleven years old. I was still hanging out with my friends and talking about girls' stuff and I liked boys but the whole concept of getting my first kiss was a big deal or holding some-body's hand was a big deal. There's a whole lot of sex going on with kids nowadays. So I think a lot of kids are feeling like they need to grow up really fast, especially girls, they need to have the breasts, they need to have the body, they need to act like a woman even though they don't really know how it is to be a woman. And I think that's the most difficult thing about being a girl now because there's no go outside and play with the Barbie dolls or just kick it with your girls anymore. It's none of that anymore. It's this whole thing about I have to like a boy. I have to do this with a boy, or I have to present myself this way. There's this whole emphasis on sex. (program coordinator)

Teenage sex, for Maya, was a recent phenomenon and specific to this genera-tion. Youth today were forced to grow up too fast. For, unlike her generation, those who were just talking about "girl stuff" and playing with Barbie dolls, these young women were engaging in "womanly" acts without having the benefit of a "womanly mind." During this interview, the issue of teen sexuality was a common thread that ran throughout all of Maya's answers. In fact, teen sex served as *the* signifying mark for the younger generation of girls she served and was a critical line of demarcation between GEP girls and the women of her generation.

Maya felt the media were fueling and reinforcing this focus on sex. When asked "What is it like being a young African American or Black girl today?" she replied:

> It can be pretty difficult. Just because we're coming up in this time of TV and everybody's watching TV and everybody's looking at all these images portrayed on the television and they feel like they need to like fall into these images. So I think a lot of girls feel like they have to have the clothes, have the hair, have this certain image of you know they're not necessarily fast, but you know they're hip to what's going on. I think for a lot of girls, especially the ones that I see, it's really difficult cuz a lot of them aren't like that. (program coordinator, age twenty-three)

According to Maya, girls had to be "not necessarily fast—but hip to what's going on." That is, girls were supposed to be worldly but not experienced. They were supposed to be sexy, "put themselves out there," but allow the male to initiate sexual activity.

Yasmine agreed. She said:

> I think we're going through another sexual revolution. Sexuality is being defined and the information and what young girls have to deal with almost from the time they are erect and say a sentence is more than would've ever came into my eleven-year-old brain. I would've never even gone there. To have all that information around the sex act, not necessarily sexuality. So the challenge is having that information and what to do with it. So much of it is how we define who we are. (program coordinator, age thirty)

It was within the context of the explosion of hip-hop culture and increased media access that the staff's Africentric womanist articulation of sexual agency must be understood. Negotiating the dominant stereotypes of welfare queen and teen mom and the indigenous representations of "bitches" and gold diggers, as well as the realities of early motherhood, sexual abuse, and violence within the girls' lives, was complex and oftentimes contradictory. For these women who grew up on R&B and what I'll call first-wave hip-hop, where women were still fly girls, sexuality was a minefield with few safe spaces.[1] Sex, sexuality, and reproduction were complicated and overlapping sites that were best captured through a discourse of control.

Located within this terrain, sexual agency was understood first and foremost as "ownership" and control over one's body. Maya noted:

> I think I'm always putting out there. I think all of us are always talking about valuing yourself as a young lady, valuing your body, owning . . . being an owner of who you are and not letting people control you, being in control of you. (program coordinator, age twenty-three)

Similarly, Yasmine reflected:

> . . . even as far as sex. And we tell the kids that . . . I'm going to do this, but I'm going to control this. I'm not going to let it interfere with my life. (program coordinator, age thirty)

As noted earlier, Black women's and girls' location within the current race-gender hierarchy makes them vulnerable to sexual violence, economic exploitation, and social control (Davis 1981; Collins 1991). This emphasis on control and ownership of self and one's body was rooted in GEP women's own fears based upon Black women's historical experiences, the staff's present and past, as well as the present-day realities for GEP girls. Ananda noted:

> It's scary because—well, one, you know, as women we deal with—I mean, we've got our own memories of being sexual—you know, victims sexually in terms of, you know, the object of somebody's sick fantasy. Some man, some whoever, some adult person. . . . There's just our concern for safety for a girl, cuz you know . . . we definitely don't want her to be sexually abused, you know, or have anything done to her that was not her consent you know, that she didn't agree to. (dance instructor, age thirty-five)

Clearly one strand of this fear was grounded in the realities of Black women's and girls' sexual victimization. It addressed the day-to-day struggles of GEP girls who were sexually assaulted in their homes and school. It also spoke to the realities of Sun Valley, where young women had been kidnapped and raped as well as victimized in a series of home invasion rapes and robberies.[2]

In addition, GEP staff members were deeply concerned about the complicated sexual politics in play within Sun Valley. They were especially concerned about trickin', "the practice of using sex or the suggestion of sex as a bartering chip" to get the right clothes, get your hair and/or nails done, keep food on the table and/or a roof over your head, as well as secure protection from sexual harassment and perhaps even assault from other men (Morgan 1999, 198). While trickin' is something women across all socioeconomic and racial groups practice and "lives on because of the patriarchal imbalance of power," poverty lays bare the rawness of this exchange (Morgan 1999, 199). For GEP women, trickin' represented an unfair exchange, one in which girls often ended up losing control over their bodies, their sexuality, their reproductive choices, and at times their lives. GEP staff feared that girls, who were often struggling financially and in need of protection on the streets, would be both attracted to and exploited by older "boys" in the community who had money and strong street reputations. They also feared that if GEP girls were not shown alternative ways to gain power, protection, financial security, and social mobility that they would willingly participate in this exchange.

Teen pregnancy was perhaps the staff's biggest fear. Staff's speculations on the causes of teen pregnancy and early motherhood included the following: inadequate sex education; lack of access to birth control; inconsistent use of birth control; complicated gender norms that made it difficult for "good girls" to prepare and plan for sex; coercive sexual relationships; the desire for autonomy or adult status; the desire for an emotional attachment, either from the father and/or the child; poor self-esteem; and lack of power. Ultimately, within GEP, girls' pregnancies were often understood as a loss of control and as a failure to determine their own future. In no uncertain terms, Maya stated:

> A successful GEP girl is one who doesn't get pregnant, who can critically think out situations. So even if she is choosing to have sexual intercourse, that she is taking action to keep herself from getting pregnant. (program coordinator, age twenty-three)

Ife recounted:

> For a long time I demonized the teen mom . . . I got pregnant as a teenager. I chose not to have a child. My life would have been completely different. . . . Girlfriend (the figure of the teenage mother) sits there and what I understand about why I got pregnant at that time was lack of control, a lack of someone being real with me about what that prize—college—meant. . . . There is no context in this culture to be a teen mom and be safe. (executive director, age thirty-six)

For Ife, teen pregnancy, rather than being seen as a moral issue, was an issue of lack of control (power) and safety. Specifically, teen pregnancy was associated with bad economic and social outcomes. In Ife's case, it was a lack of understanding about the importance of college as a critical step in her future and the implications that motherhood had for that. In contrast to the dominant narrative of teen moms being "out of control," GEP staff understood teen pregnancy as a lack of control—specifically girls' lack of control over the sexual encounter, their reproductive choices and future. This understanding was transferred to GEP girls.

With regards to girls' outcomes, Cheryl reflected:

> In my experience if it is a pregnancy prevention program there is this . . . mentality that it is not acceptable and not OK and if it does happen there are all these kinds of reasons it happened, like the family, she was pressured, all these excuses for it. . . . I think it's hard because we know that our girls are having sex, that their peers are having sex, and not that we are not mature enough to have those conversations, because we are talking about it, but we are talking about it like it's bad and I think that it's hard to talk about because we don't want to glamorize how important sexuality is so instead of talking about it in and of itself, we want to prevent that outcome. . . . We think talking about it gives it power. (program coordinator, age twenty-five)

Despite staff's desire to celebrate the "creativity," "beauty," and power of pregnancy and motherhood, they felt they could not celebrate this transition fully because they did not want to "glamorize" or "encourage" early motherhood for fear of "bad outcomes" such as dropping out of high school, welfare dependency, limited job opportunities, lack of a college education, and overall financial hardship. In other words, despite their knowledge that poverty was a predictor of teen pregnancy, staff saw girls' pregnancies as the "final nail in the coffin." In their view, early motherhood made it almost impossible for a girl to "get out" of Sun Valley.

Moreover, as a result of dominant society's interpretation of teen pregnancy, both as lack of control and lack of morality, any expression of girls' sexuality set into motion a fear of GEP losing its reputation and possibly funding. As Monica made clear, "There is a certain level of blame that people will put on us for havin' them girls getting' pregnant" (GEP intern, age eighteen). Similarly, Jamila responded, "I feel like in the organization it feels like a failure, GEP is not doing their job because girls are still getting pregnant" (program assistant, age twenty).

Teen pregnancy was GEP's pink elephant. It contained key issues around sexuality, self-sufficiency/dependency, and reproduction that the organization was attempting to challenge and move against. Its presence or even the hint of it—as visualized through girls' dance—strained internal and external relationships and pushed up against the staff's understanding of sexual agency and the organization's ideal of Africentric womanist femininity. As a result, while the articulation of Africentric womanist femininity was supposed to represent an assertion of autonomy, it set into place an ordering or hierarchy of Black femininities that marginalized other representations of Black womanhood.

AFRICENTRIC WOMANISM AS A "POLITICS OF RESPECTABILITY"

Now when we say Africentric we mean this. . . . If you disagree with these definitions you can choose to be in another organization with different definitions. At the same time, I really do want folks to have space to disagree, but I need for us to get on the same page. (Ife, as quoted in Gamble and Associates 1999, 12)

Within GEP, the deployment of an Africentric womanist femininity became a "politics of respectability." That is, on the one hand, staff's Africentric womanist femininity functioned as a racialized gender strategy that attempted to destabilize the cultural representations that justified and normalized the practices that unfairly penalized Black women. On the other hand, Africentric womanist femininity came to be an ordering principle, creating distinctions between what were considered appropriate and inappropriate displays of Black femininity, especially Black female sexuality. That is, GEP staff used the themes of self-definition, self-determination, and sexual agency to construct a "standard" against which Black womanness was judged. Black femininities became stratified, and Africentric womanist femininity was the ideal to which all others had to conform.

For GEP staff, Africentric womanist femininity was embodied in the lyrics and public persona of Lauryn Hill, the female vocalist of the Fugees, a popular 1990s hip-hop group and subsequently a solo artist who garnered international acclaim. Hill was a self-determining, self-defining, self-loving, and powerful woman. Following in the footsteps of Queen Latifah, Salt-n-Pepa, MC Lyte and Monie Love, she presented an "Afro-femme regality, refined sensuality and womanist strength" (Morgan 1999, 199). Yasmine reflected:

I really like Lauryn Hill, and I think she puts out a really positive image. . . . I think now there's sort of coming to be a proud Black woman figure out there in a lot of ways. Culturally aware, intelligent, and still able—not like "bourgie"—still able to communicate on the level but like speaking real, speaking reality. . . . And hopefully this is a trend that is growing and we can get away from these Foxy Browns, X Prostitutes, and Lil' Kims. (program coordinator, age thirty)

Hill's lyrics and public persona were not just embraced by GEP women. She and Erykah Badu were praised by the black media

for their mixture of Afrocentric/Rastafarian/Five-Percenter ideology and "old-school" credibility. Badu and Hill became exemplars of the "purist" revival against "negative" female artists like Lil' Kim and have been particularly lauded for dressing and acting with self-respect and dignity. (Baldwin 2004, 175)

For GEP staff and many other Black men and women, Lauryn Hill was the hip-hop star who young girls could look up to. She carried herself with pride and projected an image of a powerful woman that "knew how to act."

GEP constructed the figures of Foxy Brown and Lil' Kim as the oppositional pair to Hill and Badu. Lil' Kim (aka Kimberly Jones) and Foxy Brown (aka Inga Marchard) are female rap artists who have "lyrical personas of hyper-sexed, couture-clad hoochie mamas" and "represent the punanny-for-sale materialism" (Morgan 1999, 199). Lil' Kim and Foxy Brown explicitly celebrated trickin', often rapping about their ability to access men's wealth, power, and prestige by allowing sexual access to their bodies. Their lyrics and onstage personas highlight masculinity's dependence on access to and control over women and how women's control over the "punanny" provides women with a valuable bargaining chip (Morgan 1999, 199).

For Yasmine, a self-described "child of the 1970s," the explosion of rap music and music videos onto the scene in the 1980s and 1990s created a qualitative change in the way young women negotiated and expressed their sexuality. She said this:

Girls today are exposed to way more sex and violence, and not only in reality like in their everyday lives, but also in the media. So the videos that they're watching, the music that they're listening to, the magazines that they're reading are filled with images of women that are just very very sexual, and this is what they are learning from. It is just so acceptable to be basically naked. The clothes that they wear are overtly sexual; expose a lot of their breasts and rears. And the roles that they are in . . . the relationship between a man and a woman, as far as the music industry is concerned, is a strictly sexual relationship. That's what I'm seeing in posters, pictures, always the women, you know, bent over, just used as these *sexual tools.* (program coordinator, age thirty)

The concept of being a sexual tool was important for Yasmine, and she returned to it repeatedly throughout our conversation. The concept served to describe this shift in sexuality, which, according to Yasmine, was embodied in the personas of Lil' Kim and Foxy Brown. She explained:

We were taking pictures for the slide show. Some of the poses that the girls were standing in to take this picture were straight from a Foxy Brown album cover. One girl, I had to keep telling her to pull her shirt down because she was trying to stand so that her full belly could be exposed. At face value there is nothing wrong with her skin showing, but I could see that behind that there was so much more. It meant something. If her shirt was just up I probably wouldn't have tripped, but it was saying something else. She was trying to say something else. . . . To me it was about, I don't know, it was just this overt sexuality. . . . I don't even know the word for it. There was a whole attitude that came along with that . . . this cheapened sort of . . . there's a whole other mentality, like, "It's all good." It is more than, you know, I want to flirt with you, I want to get to know you. It's more on the level of, "Let's do it." It's just sex—not, "I want to get your attention and maybe we can hang out." Strictly sex. That's the energy I'm feeling that these girls are picking up from these images . . . it bothers me. (program coordinator, age thirty)

While Yasmine clearly struggled to come up with the words to adequately describe what she was seeing, she was very clear that the overt display of Black female sexuality bothered her. In addition, it was the "strictly sex" energy represented by these figures of Foxy Brown and Lil' Kim that caused her concern.

Lil' Kim's and Foxy Brown's "in your face" sexuality and their trickin' mentality, for Yasmine, did not reflect sexual liberation on the part of Black woman. In fact, Yasmine asserted, "Somebody made the assumption that they were redefining sexuality for women, and I don't agree with that" (program coordinator, age thirty).

Cheryl complicated the analysis. She reflected:

> I think there is some power associated with it; they are making money and money means a lot and when you have your own money you are supposed to provide for what you need and want. . . . So in a sense they have power. I definitely think it's money power they have, and say-so about fashion and what is cute. They set trends and the power that their words have. And smaller children, five to six, will know every word to these songs, but not necessarily know how to read or write. So when they talk about having people know your name and reputation, how valued that is, that is power, too, but she's not changing the world, making it any better for women and girls, making it so we are getting more respect. I feel like she's normalizing that whole image that it's cool to exploit yourself to get what you need and if that is what you have to do then that is what you have to do. (program coordinator, age twenty-five)

Cheryl maintained that Foxy Brown and Lil' Kim were complex figures. On the one hand, they had power. They had money, so they were models of self-sufficiency. They came off as women in control—assertive and sexually assured. They also had the power of recognition and the power of their voice heard and immortalized on wax.

In Cheryl's opinion, however, while Foxy Brown and Lil' Kim might have had power, it did not translate into "respect" for women and girls. Instead, their "in your face sexuality" was understood as normalizing women's exploitation of self for money, power, and prestige. In other words, their presentation of "sexual freedom is illusory" (Sharpley-Whiting 2007, 66). Although they may have reclaimed their sexuality and celebrated women's erotic pleasure, by commodifying their pleasure, they reproduced the patriarchal system and ultimately men's control (see Watts 2002).[3] In this way, Foxy Brown and Lil' Kim, representatives of the "sexual tool" mentality, were poor models of Black womanhood, because they were "depending on their sexuality to get the attention and power that they need. They're saying, "Look at me. I'm this sexual being and that's all I am" (Yasmine, program coordinator, age thirty). For GEP women, this represented a condition of low self-esteem and internalized oppression.

Thus echoing their nineteenth-century foremothers, their position was, "If you want to combat whatever, then you need to portray yourself in a way that combats it . . . not take it on, not become this thing" (Yasmine, program coordinator, age thirty). In other words, they did not "subscribe to the whole idea that if I take over this word or this idea, I'm taking away your power to harm me with it" (Yasmine, program coordinator, age thirty).

GEP women recognized the external forces that impinged upon Black women to limit their choices. Yasmine added:

> I know that like in history that . . . traditionally our sexuality has been taken away from us. Portrayed as ugly, unattractive, and fat and whatever else. And so I sorta understand the need. I guess. I just believe it is the *wrong approach*. (program coordinator, age thirty)

Their goal was to

> . . . help them [the girls] realize they're more than that. To realize that they are also smart and creative, talented people. And they have a lot more value than whatever that sexual aspect is. And . . . when these . . . girls know that they're more than, they're way more than this body part, and that you have all these other things to offer, they won't want to be seen as just a body part. They'll be like, "Look at me. I'm smart. I have a lot to say, I have something to say." So that won't even come into play. I mean they'll still be feminine, sexual beings, but they'll do, be, in the *right way*. (Yasmine, program coordinator, age thirty)

As the phrases "wrong approach" and "right way" indicate, the ranking of Black femininities was clear. Africentric womanist femininity became a politics of respectability.

Historically, respectability embodied moral authority and "placed women at the center of the discursive construction," such that morality and, hence, respectability are thought to be readable off/observable from the bodies of women (Finch 1993). At the core of respectability discourses are normative notions of sexuality. Within the United States, working-class and Black femininities have been constructed as "authentically" or "innately" "pathological, polluting, and poisonous" and otherwise disreputable—without respect (Skeggs 1997, 13). To counter this characterization, GEP women identified sexual agency as sexual control. For these women, an Africentric womanist femininity distanced them from hypersexualized representations of Black femininity. These women performed respectability via constructing themselves as self-defined, self-determined agents of their sexuality. In other words, GEP women expressed their racialized gender identity by deliberately attempting *not* to be the stereotyped welfare queen, "trick" or "ho" broadcast in popular culture. They dis-identified (Skeggs 1997). This process of dis-identification supported the development of a hierarchy of Black femininities within the organization. With this hierarchy in place, GEP women marginalized different versions of Black femininity, especially those that contained competing discourses regarding sex and sexuality.

GEP GIRLS' DECENT GIRL FEMININITY

At GEP's fifth anniversary event, the girls performed the poem "A Great Somebody," written by Adrian Sceley Hartesty. Performed with movement, in a call-and-response fashion, the girls declared:

I am	I am
a great somebody	a great somebody
start teaching me now	start teaching me now
start leading me now	start leading me now
start guiding me now	start guiding me now
start praising me now	start praising me now
and you will see us r . . . i . . . s . . . e to the top	

This was a performances that I will always remember. I immediately got that feeling—when you get goose bumps and your eyes tear up, and you know that everyone in the room is having that same response. It was the girls' owning of the poem and the emotional urgency in their voices that moved me. Their voices insisted that they "were somebody" and demanded that they be heard. Later I came to learn that this desire to be seen and to be heard as somebody formed the foundation of their decent girl femininity.

It is important to note that GEP girls did not enter the program as "blank slates" waiting to absorb GEP's Africentric womanist femininity. They brought their emergent racialized gender consciousness and thoughts about "how to be" women into the program. For example, when asked "What are the biggest problems facing young girls today?" girls responded:

Some of the stuff that starts happening at my school is that the boys start liking girls and the girls start liking boys. Then the boys wanna have sex with the girls. When they get finished messing around with the girls they tell each other, "ahh nigga you tight for that," and they say this to the girls "you a nasty a—b—," and all these bad names to the girls. The treatment between boys and girls is so different. (Stephanie, GEP girl, age thirteen)

Being an African American girl is hard, because in school the teacher immediately assumes we are bad and have no manners before we can show them what or who we really are and can do. I am an African American girl struggling to be somebody. (Tracy, GEP girl, age sixteen)

A black woman actually has a voice that has a life of its own. Now either two things can happen. Either you can grow up and end up in a position where that voice has been hidden and put away—that the soul behind the voice is suppressed. I don't want to say poverty but just like . . . being an inner-city youth often causes us to distort that soul. . . . Because what happens is we are introduced to things like the media and other people . . . and through those things we pick up our own notions and other people's notions about how we are supposed to act, versus how we think we should act or whatever. (Nyema, GEP girl and intern, age seventeen)

Growing up a woman in society is kind of hard, but after awhile you get used to it. . . . Today we just want society to treat us just like everybody else, we want to be able to do what a man can do without being called a "Dyke" or lesbian. . . . Being a minority woman is hard. I have to admit that I live my life against all odds and try not to fall victim to the stereotypes that have been set out there for me to fall into. . . . We most of the time come from poor families, so they figure we are automatic failures, nobody wants to give us a chance; they think you will never be nothing. Now with the government having that type of attitude towards my culture and my gender I will never have equal opportunity. (Olivia, GEP girl, age sixteen)

GEP girls were already familiar with the challenges facing Black women and girls. These barriers, both small and large, informed their understanding of the world in which they lived but also shaped their notions of what kind of woman they wanted and needed to be to survive and thrive in such a world.

During the 1960s, Joyce Ladner (1972) set about describing and analyzing "what approaching womanhood meant to poor black girls in the city" (1). Ladner found that Black girls typically relate to one of four constructions of Black womanhood: the traditional Black woman, the laissez-faire egalitarian woman, the middle-class woman, and the powerless woman. The dominant model, according to Ladner, was the traditional Black woman, which referred to the "stable and hardworking" woman who took a "strong role in the family" (131). The laissez-faire model represented a "fun-loving and somewhat carefree model" that addressed girls' desire to be released from the "constraints and pressures" identified with the traditional model (138). The third construction, the middle-class Black woman, was made up of three parts, according to Ladner: a commitment to education, a desire to leave the community, and a conformist attitude to dominant expectations of White middle-class women (140). Finally, the fourth model represented the power-less woman or the "transplanted plantation girl" in terms of "economic, social, and political oppression" (169). This construction of Black femininity addressed those women and girls who tried and gave up on the "good life," and those who never dared to dream of such a life. While time and place have transformed the models of womanhood to which "poor black girls in the city" aspire, core elements of Ladner's constructions remain.

GEP Girls were keenly aware of the spectrum of models available to them and clearly rejected the powerless model. For example, in response to the question, "Are there women that you definitely don't want to be like?," Rolanda described a character from a movie:

> This lady on the movie was like . . . I'm a hoochie, I wear hoochie clothes, and one day she got raped and she started selling her body and she had a baby and didn't know what to do. So she put her baby in the dumpster and a truck came and got it and the truck almost killed her baby. I don't want to be like that. (GEP girl, age eleven)

Other responses to the question were: "Drug addicts, pregnant teens, alco-holics" (Kisha, GEP girl, age sixteen); "Billie Holiday" (Malika, GEP girl, age twelve); "Drugs, hanging on the corner in the street everyday, got a lot of babies" (Marlene, GEP girl, age eleven). GEP girls did not want to be drug addicts, victims of sexual violence, prostitutes, or young mothers.

Instead, like most of the girls in Ladner's (1972) study, they wanted to be somebody. When asked to imagine yourself at age twenty-one, GEP girls responded:

> I'm going to college, and another college, and another college. I'm living in Oakland. I have no children. I'm not married. I'm driving a red car, a limousine. I never plan on having children. (Jamaica, age eight)

> Working as a physical therapist, no kids, staying with my mom, trying to find me a place. (Aneshia, age thirteen)

> A good job, I got my own house, no kids, working in the law field. (Tangee, age sixteen)

> I'm working at an office in computers. I'm living in a nice neighbor-hood in Bay City. I'm getting to work by car, a Jetta. I don't have

any kids, not married, have a boyfriend. For fun, I go out with my friends. (Mekka, age ten)

I'm going to college, then I'm gonna be a photographer and then I'm going to photographer school and then I'm going to take pictures of models. I'm gonna live in L.A. and take pictures of mansions and stuff and take pictures for *People* magazine. I'm not married, no children, maybe a man. I'm driving a Mercedes. (Lauren, age eleven)

I'm not living here or in California. I'm moving away to Egypt, no, I'm not moving there because there's no Nikes and no McDonald's. I'm tired of Bay City. . . . I'm gonna be in college, not married, no kids. I'm in college studying design and making a lot of money. (Diamond, age twelve)

Having a job and got a car. I'm a teacher and I'm driving a Legend. I'm living in Sacramento, because it's quiet. I probably have one child. I'm not married. For fun I go to play games, go to parties, still like I was a kid. I'll be around twenty-five when I have my first child. Probably not earlier because I won't be ready for kids. (Malika, age twelve)

I'm going to college. I'm working on getting my degree and I already have my car. I'll be rolling in a Lexus. I don't have any kids. I don't really want no kids. Yes, I have a man. My sister and brother have kids. I'm gonna watch their kids as doing them a favor, but not all the time. I got plans to do, people to see, and places to go. (Rolanda, age eleven)

Not one girl I interviewed stated that she wanted to be married or have children as a young mother. In fact, they all adamantly spoke against this reality. Children and marriage represented a detour off the path they envisioned for themselves—a detour away from the "somebody" that these young women imagined themselves becoming. This "somebody" brought together Ladner's laissez-faire, traditional, and middle-class versions of Black femininity and exposed GEP girls' own model of Black femininity: a working-class femininity grounded in what Anderson (1999) calls a "decent" orientation.

As noted earlier, many working-class and poor residents draw distinctions between those families and individuals who are "decent" and those who are street. According to Anderson (1999), those youth with a decent orientation are committed to middle-class values of hard work, education, and respectability. GEP girls imagined themselves as decent young women. They wanted an education, in particular, a college education; they wanted to leave Sun Valley—both physically and metaphorically; they wanted to delay motherhood; and they wanted to have fun. In other words, despite popular constructions as being deviant and outside of society's norms, GEP girls were clearly part of the mainstream. They uncritically embraced the achievement ideology and understood education as their vehicle out of Sun Valley and up the road to economic social mobility. Girls also understood having children as an impediment along this path. Jamaica and Rolanda even declared that they did not want children, while others spoke of waiting until they were ready for kids. Girls also adamantly asserted that they would not be married. They saw themselves as independent, self-reliant, educated, upwardly mobile professional women who knew how to enjoy life.

Key to understanding their vision of a "decent girl" from Sun Valley was their definition of "ghetto," or what Anderson would describe as "street." For example, when asked why they attended GEP instead of the neighborhood Boys and Girls Club, GEP girls responded:

I don't like that Boys and Girls Club. They just be fighting and ghetto cussin' and stuff . . . I don't like it because there's a lot of ghetto children down there. They always talk about people, fight people. That's why GEP is better than that. (Diamond, age twelve)

They don't have to do homework there, they can curse and fight, they can do anything. (Jamaica, age eight)

It's too off-the-hook. It's too much confusion, too loud. I would still come here if my mom said I could go there or here. (Zoë, age ten)

The girls that go there flirt, and pop their butts in front of the boys. The reason why I come here, because if I go to the Boys and Girls Club I get into some drama with the mess they got down there. (Rolanda, age eleven)

I got a few friends that live in Sun Valley. They don't come to GEP, they like to hang in Sun Valley more than they like the after-school program. I try to get them to go, but they don't want to, so oh well. They just hang on the corner and talk. I don't do that because my momma don't let me go around a lot of ghetto people, hanging on the corner, 'cause she don't want me getting into anything. . . .

People in my family think (GEP's) cool cause they keep us here and
not in the streets. (Malika, age twelve)

Sun Valley girls chose GEP because within it there were not a lot of "ghetto
children," and "ghetto" behavior was not allowed.

GEP girls were very aware of the representations of poor Black girls
within mainstream discourses. Similar to GEP women, they too worked to
distance themselves from "the loud and overtly sexualized" image of Black
girls. In this way, being ghetto or "playing outside," "flirting," and "poppin'
your butts in front of the boys" were understood to be "inappropriate" ways
to be a decent girl. Expressions of sexuality and violence were at the center
of this ghetto girl construction.

In addition, and in contrast to some of the staff's assumptions, GEP girls
also had very little respect for Lil' Kim or Foxy Brown. Eleven-year-old Carol
responded, "I think they're nasty because Lil' Kim be in the magazine and
she don't have no clothes on, not even a bra and she just be covering her
nipples" (GEP girl). Similarly, sixteen-year-old Kisha reflected, "They give
their body out too much, the things she say and do and I can't see myself
doing that" (GEP girl). Routinely described as "nasty," girls placed them with
prostitutes and identified them as undesirable models for their future selves.
Taken together, they commanded little respect. Nyema agreed, saying:

They present themselves as women with low standards around men
. . . around sexual activity. Sleeping with men for money. You know,
sleeping with men so that they can break bread. . . . The decision
comes from, from seeing wealth, from seeing immediate gratification
and wanting that. From greed, from deceit. . . . They, they kind of, I
want to say impair or they kind of—they damage. They damage the
black girls' view of morals, of values. If I were Lil' Kim I would have
a serious problem with my history. You know that streetwalkin',
that's not—I mean come on, it's not OK. And then to rap about it
as though it's glorious and, that makes you "tight." Why do you
have to disrespect yourself, call yourself out your name in order to
be bad? In order to say, "I'm strong. I don't need a man, I'm gonna
get what I want." You don't have to degrade yourself and disrespect
your culture and who you are just to make money and just to prove
that point. (GEP girl and intern, age seventeen)

According to Nyema, Lil' Kim and Foxy Brown represented a Black femininity that "damages Black girls' view of moral and values." Specifically, they
presented "low standards around men and sexual activity" that "disrespect"
their culture and "degrade" themselves.

Instead, GEP girls wanted to be a different kind of woman. They too admired Lauryn Hill. Nyema reflected:

> I think now there are role models. We've got Lauryn Hill, we've got Erykah Badu. Erykah Badu and Lauryn Hill, I would say, are sort of a reflection of that Afrocentric nature. . . . The focus with Lauryn Hill and Erykah Badu is more so on the exterior and how they, how they care for their interior, how they care for themselves and their hearts. They are . . . black women who are independent and you know really positive factors in society. You can understand where they're coming from. . . . They portray images of women I wouldn't mind being. (GEP girl and intern, age seventeen)

This celebration of Hill, which corresponded to the release of her multi-platinum album *The Miseducation of Lauryn Hill*, was evident in GEP's public performances and group sessions. Girls selected her music to accompany their dance routines. They discussed her songs during group, and, during the summer of 2000, they created a video of their lives, given voice, if you will, by Hill's lyrics in *Every Ghetto, Every City*:

> I was just a little girl
> Skinny legs and press and curl
> My mother always thought I'd be a star
> But way before my record deal,
> The streets that nurtured Lauryn Hill
> Made sure that I'd never go too far . . .
> Every Ghetto, Every City, Every Suburban Place I've Been
> Make Me Recall the Days Back in New Jerusalem
> Looking Back. . . .[4]

The video captured girls in their homes, on the playground, and even on the bus. Girls were seen on those rare hot summer days in Bay City, sitting outside eating popsicles and combing each other's hair. Hill's lyrics provided the context for witnessing the everyday moments of the girls' reality and gave a clear sense of who these young women were and who they wanted to be. This was a moment when both GEP women and girls could come together in agreement. Hill's public persona and her lyrics were both read and accepted as an embodiment of an Africentric womanist femininity and young women's decent working-class femininity.

GEP girls' ideas about "what to do" and "how to be" a decent Black girl mapped onto the Africentric womanist femininity practiced within GEP.

Their construction relied heavily on middle-class notions of education, self-determination, and appropriate sexuality. Consider Nyema's response:

> I just think a successful GEP girl is a young lady. Someone who is a positive role model, whether she has a child at an early age. If so, she's someone who doesn't find herself (I think it's an important thing) in subsidized housing. I'm sorry. That's down on the ghetto, but it's a trap. There's a door that closes, and it's hard to open. And being a GEP girl, you should be enlightened to the illnesses that our kids catch from birth living here. A healthy, successful GEP girl wouldn't have a child before she was truly ready. A successful GEP girl has a plan. College is a good plan because it gives you more time to think of a better plan. She makes conscious decisions. . . . She may not be having sex, but she knows that it exists and what the repercussions are, the pros and cons. . . . She is responsible. . . . She's independent. (GEP girl and intern, age seventeen)

Regarding sex and early motherhood, Kisha noted:

> Females tell me they got to have sex, and some females be like sex "I did it once and I don't feel it and I ain't doing it again." Some females get peer pressure, or they feel it's the right time. But me, I feel I can wait, I'm not in a rush and I want to be old enough to take care of a baby. I want to have my stuff packed and know that if I have a baby I know I can do this for it, have a house, you feel me. I don't want to be moving here today, then there, got not clothes, no money, no food. I want to have all that down in a situation. I don't want to be asking people for things. That's not me. I want to do things on my own. If I really need it, I'll ask you. But I really like being independent through my own self. (GEP girl, age sixteen)

Africentric womanist themes of self-determination, sexual agency (as sexual control, especially control over reproduction), and self-definition were not antithetical to the underlying themes within the girls' own definition of Black femininity. This matching of ideologies was a result of GEP girls' self-selection into the program. As noted earlier, the girls had four other free neighborhood programs from which they could choose. The girls chose GEP because it corresponded to their own visions of "how to be" a decent Black girl.

GEP was constructed as a safe place for these particular girls to explore alternative versions of femininity that spoke to what they wanted in life.

Nyema noted: "GEP helped me to feel comfortable with who I am. I didn't have to conform to anyone's idea of what a black 13-year-old should be" (as quoted in Wagner 1998). Nyema made it clear that a critical component of GEP girls' success was being able to make "the journey away from "other people's notions of how we are supposed to act" and toward their own voice. For other Sun Valley girls who claimed a "decent Black girl identity, GEP presented them with a version of Black femininity that they could potentially use to achieve their own goals of social mobility.

For example, as part of GEP's five-year anniversary event, girls wrote essays or letters to Black heroines such as Rosa Parks, Harriet Tubman, Sojourner Truth, and Alice Walker. They also wrote to GEP staff. For example:

> Dear Danielle,
> I am writing to you to tell you about my life and where I come from. Being a girl is important to me because I get to come to GEP. GEP is an important part of my life. I love to come to GEP because the people there care for us and help us when we need help. I admire you because you are the Shimmershine Queen. You are nice and you take me places. You give me ideas like thinking positively and treating people like I want to be treated. I know that I can be the best student if I have a good attitude and if I am a leader not a follower. You give me ideas from your heart when I am very sad, and when I feel lost you help me. You give me hints because you want me to graduate from the eighth grade and you are going to help me so I can be successful in my life. I will always remember you forever. (Diamond, age twelve)

> Dear Danielle,
> I am writing to you because I want to tell you about myself and what is important to me. I admire you because you are nice and caring. You are responsible for yourself and giving. You help me with my homework when I need help. You are a hard-working person. You buy me things when I have good grades. You let me have anything I need. You are special. I am special too. I am special because I am nice and caring. I work hard in school. I share with others. I help others when they need help. I have the key to the successful life in my hand. (Cathy, age eleven)

> Dear Sister Aisha,
> I am writing to you to tell you about myself, how I live and about my future. The reason I admire you is because you are a great

person to look up to. You are a great and fun group leader. (Vicki, age twelve)

GEP girls found that GEP staff modeled a Black femininity that could support them toward their own path out of Sun Valley. As noted earlier, many GEP staff did not have easy lives. Many experienced poverty, early pregnancies, and temporary homelessness, yet despite these difficulties, GEP women were not powerless or exploited victims. With regard to GEP women, Yasmine, a program coordinator for the older girls, noted:

I mean, we all have our issues. We all grew up Black and women, young girls. I think we try to teach them, and how we come at them is definitely on the level they can relate to. I don't think we keep our lives so hidden from them that we put ourselves on this pedestal and it's like, "OK, you need to grow up and be like us." I think they see us struggling to find housing or whatever. I think that we are real people and we come across to them as real people and at the same time we are Black women who have worked and struggled and are still struggling . . . but basically we have ourselves together. And we're letting them know that you can do it. It's not going to be easy but you can do it. Here we are . . . I'm not on welfare. I may be totally different from what they're used to. And even the fact that I'm not living in the projects, I'm not on welfare says something to them. I don't have to live in a big house or drive a fancy car, the fact is I have a car . . . we're so opposite of "bourgie." Our lives in general, the way we are, what we experience, what we're going through we can't be "bourgie" because our connection with these girls is too close for us even to pretend like we're something higher than what we are. (age thirty)

Thus GEP girls were able to map their own decent girl femininity onto GEP's Africentric womanist femininity. However, as will be explored in the next chapter in greater detail, it was the girls' close agreement with self-definition and self-determination that complicated their acceptance of GEP's definition of sexual agency.

6

Dance Lessons

At Sun Valley's multicultural community celebration, another conflict erupted over representations of Black womanhood as presented and read through GEP girls' dancing. Leslie, a staff member, recounted the event:

> So what happened is the girls were asked to dance at the community event and they were given two days to prepare. So the girls worked really hard for the two days to prepare and learn this dance. They really came together and did a great job. What happened is everything was really cool, except at one part, at the very end they got in a circle and a couple of girls did the "booty dance," but we said, "Uh uh!" But the day of the show, instead of two girls doing the "booty dance," they all did the booty dance—and instead of their booties facing each other, they were in a U and their booties faced the audience. After that it was like community anger, or disappointment, and people from different community agencies said, "That's not GEP! What were those girls doing? What's your new staff teaching them?" In fact, Ife ended up crying about the incident because there was so much community reaction to the event. (program coordinator, age twenty-seven)

Roberta, a GEP mother, remembered:

> I was at the community multicultural thing and I looked and I could not believe it, and was so glad that Zoë (her daughter) did not

dance with them. But when I seen them doing that—they were rep-resenting us and them dancing like that . . . oohh, Chinese people sitting there, you could tell it was not appropriate for where they were, it was OK at a club or something, but, "Oh, no." One parent asked me, she said she heard some people were complaining, and she asked me what I thought, and I told her I was sitting in the front and I was through! She said, "I don't want to talk bad about the program, but it wasn't appropriate." So I seen Ife and she started crying because some parents called and were complaining about the way they were dancing. (mother of GEP girl, age twenty-seven)

Ten-year-old Zoë reflected:

I think it was just because . . . most people were doing something based on a culture and GEP was just expressing themselves and it made them stand out. There was these other people from Sun Valley that were doing the Wild Wild West, and it was similar to what GEP was doing but it didn't have as much action as GEP's did. (GEP girl)

Roxanne, GEP's administrative director, in conversation with a potential participant's mother, had the following conversation:

She said she was questioning GEP because she was at the multicul-tural event and GEP girls did their hoochie dance. Then she ques-tioned the staff. Then we are back to that thing again, even though we know what they do whether they are performing or not, that is not what people want to see, even though every person that saw it has seen it before. It's the real world, but people don't want it put in their faces. . . . For me, my problem is how come the staff didn't know what these girls were doing. That bothers me, not what the girls did, but staff reaction. I feel like staff is not in control and that is what bothers me. (age fifty-four)

Finally, eleven-year-old Rolanda commented:

Say we want to do hip-hop dance, some of the dances we want to do they don't like and some of the songs they don't like. They don't like when you shaking your butt and the songs have a lot of cuss words. I think they need to get with it because some kids like all of that cussin' in the songs and all that. (GEP girl)

Once again, GEP women and girls clashed over girls' public dance performance. In this instance, GEP girls practiced one routine under the watchful
eyes of the staff and performed a more "hoochie" version at the event. From
the staff's and other community members' perspectives, GEP girls presented
or displayed an "inappropriate" image of Black femininity. Yet, as Rolanda
made clear, GEP staff and those other adults who complained "need to get
with it," because not only do girls like shaking their butts, but they *will* shake
their butts—with or without adult permission.

Dance, or the process of "speaking with your body," often served as a
public performance of GEP's identity work (Primus 1994[1998], 7). Dance
was a space in which women and girls could reclaim their bodies and remake
Black femininity. It was a space where GEP girls not only represented themselves but also the organization and Black women in general. In the words of
Roberta, a GEP mother, "They were representin' us!" Consequently, dance
performances were fraught with tension and heavily monitored to ensure an
"appropriate" public display of Black femininity.

In this chapter, I explore GEP's dance politics to critically illustrate the
negotiation over representations of Black womanhood between GEP staff
and girls. Specifically, GEP women, building upon their personal experiences
and philosophies as well as GEP's organizational power matrix, used traditional West African dance to articulate an Africentric womanist femininity
centered upon the themes of self-definition, self-reliance, and sexual
agency—often articulated as control over Black women's bodies. Alternative
Black femininities were marginalized and subordinated, thus setting up a tension within the organization between respectability and respect. This tension
became most visible through GEP girls' use of popular dance to express their
own decent girl femininity. That is, using the power they were able to mobilize through the configuration of GEP's organizational power matrix, the girls
performed popular dance moves that challenged Africentric womanist
notions of sexual agency as sexual control, especially adult control over their
bodies. As a result, they redefined and empowered themselves as Black girls
with their own unique and important identities.

THE DANCING BLACK FEMALE BODY

Think of how these cultures [Black Atlantic cultures] have used the
body—as if it was, and it often was, the only cultural capital we had.
We have worked on ourselves as the canvases of representation.
(Hall 1996, 470)

As Stuart Hall makes clear, our bodies are not simply biological phenomena. Rather, our physical bodies are encircled in a web of meaning that shapes and informs our understanding of as well as our experiences in our bodies. Moreover, such meanings identify and locate our bodies within the social hierarchy such that relations of power become inscribed onto our bodies. As a result, "Even such activities as teaching children how to move, dress, eat are thoroughly political in that they impose on them an unspoken under-standing of legitimate ways to (re) present their bodies to themselves and others" (Moi 1991, 1031).

Dance has and continues to be a critical site for representing bodies (DeFrantz 2002; Gottschild 2003). While the emphasis in dance is on the physical movement of the body, it is more than that. Dance is a cultural and political expression of the social, historical, and political contexts in which it is embedded. It is a form of social interaction intimately tied to music that has been an especially important arena for identity work. That is, dance has been a space in which to make the dancing Black female body "mean and mean again" (Hebdige 1979, 3).

AFRICAN DANCE: GEP WOMEN'S RECLAMATION OF SELF AND SEXUALITY

In her talk titled "How Black Dance Is Perceived," delivered at the Eighth Annual Conference of the International Association of Blacks in Dance, Jawole Willa Jo Zollar, choreographer and founder of The Urban Bush Woman, asserted:

> I think there comes a way that you want to reclaim your sensual being through the dance. In Nigeria, shaking the butt is raised to a powerful level of artistry. We have to work with that energy here, and raise it to a higher level so that we can begin a healing cultural momentum. (quoted in DeFrantz 2002, 24)

According to Zollar, dance provides Black women with the opportunity to "reclaim their sensual being" that has been denied to them. In particular, drawing upon Nigerian traditional dances, she identifies "shaking the butt" as a place to begin the recovery process. In other words, in contrast to the descriptions of African or Black butts as "deviant" and African dance as "licentious, savage and heathenistic" (Nettleford 1998, xv), Zollar reframes West African dance and "butt shaking" as "art."[1] Shifting to this Africanist interpretive frame, she challenges dominant codes and embarks upon the process of taking back, that which has been denied to Black women (see

Gottschild 2003). Understanding the vital role that dance plays in many African American communities and in the social life of youth, GEP women drew upon dance as a form of embodied politics to teach girls to love and respect their history, their bodies, and ultimately who they were as Black girls.

Throughout my time at GEP, I witnessed and helped coordinate several African dance performances. While girls performed African dance routines in larger venues with other youth groups at Bay City's Civic Auditorium and at local community events, African dance was the centerpiece of the program's annual Kwanzaa celebration. To prepare for this event, professional dance instructors and drummers were hired to teach the girls traditional West African dance and drumming. As part of the instruction, girls were also taught elements of West African culture, as well as the meaning of the dances and their particular movements. Over the years, girls learned and performed puberty dances, harvest celebrations, and other routines.

The period leading up to these Kwanzaa celebrations was hectic. As noted earlier, the African dance performances were part of a larger community Kwanzaa event sponsored and coordinated by GEP. Therefore, in addition to learning the dance routines, girls were often writing essays, reciting poems, rehearsing the lighting of the kinara, practicing their skits, and in general preparing for the event. During dance rehearsals the instructors, often dancers themselves, worked with the girls to master the steps as well as to express the meaning of the movements. The younger girls, those ages eight to eleven, gravitated toward African dance. After practice they would often ask the instructors, "When are you coming back?" "Can you come back tomorrow?" Perhaps it was the excitement of the new costumes, the rhythms of the drums, the ability to move their energetic and somewhat antsy bodies, and/or just the love of performing, but they often looked forward to practicing and performing. The older girls, those twelve and up, were not as enthusiastic about the dancing.[2] Instead, they seemed to enjoy drumming the most.

The performances were always amazing. While the specifics varied based upon the dance and its particular meaning, most performances began with drumming. Once the drummers introduced themselves to the audience via their respective sound and rhythm the girls, barefoot, with carefully tied African print midriff tops and coordinating raffia skirts, would enter onto the stage, most often by singing. These songs, accompanied by movement and sung in the West African language to which the dance and rhythm belonged, created the context for the dance. Once that context was set, the rhythm picked up and the girls began to "dance." As with most West African dance, the steps were strong and quick, involving bent knees, flat backs, and a series of isolations in different parts of the torso. The girls and the drummers moved like one, with each jump, shoulder shake, shimmy, and pelvic thrust synced to the rhythm. As the dance neared its end, the drummers would speed up the rhythm and the girls would dance faster and faster. At this point, the crowd would often be moved to its feet, clapping and whistling encouragement. Then with an authoritative thump from the drummers, the dance would end, and the room would fill with applause. The girls, with wide grins and oftentimes shy eyes, would bow to their audience and then to the partners, the drummers. With the performance over, they would skip, run, and hop off the stage.

For GEP women, African dance provided the girls an opportunity to re-imagine themselves outside of dominant race/gender codes reserved for Black females. Specifically, GEP women used dance to challenge the dominant standard of beauty that idealizes the White female body. Within African dance it was the varied shapes and shades of blackness that came together to create art and beauty. African dance set into motion an African aesthetic that valued and celebrated strong, assertive, and powerful Black female bodies and challenged the powerless, passive, and objectified female body emphasized in dominant culture. In other words, African dance provided an opportunity for women and girls to take on an Africentric womanist lens, to (re) imagine and (re) present Black female bodies as sites of beauty, pleasure, agency, and power.

Moreover, African dance served to separate and differentiate GEP girls from the hypersexualized stereotype of The Urban Girl, as represented by dominant society and from the images of "video hos' skeezers, and gold diggers" presented within hip-hop music and videos. That is, stripped of the objectifying lyrics found within popular music and culture and accompanied by the beats of the drums, GEP women hoped that African dance provided a space where girls could express, not objectify, themselves. This connection to their African heritage provided an opportunity for the girls to know that "when I do the nasty dance, I also know it's connected to a puberty dance" (Ife, executive director, age thirty-six). In this way, pelvic thrusts and shoulder shimmies, the same moves that often caused controversy when presented in girls' social dance routines, could be reinterpreted as affirmations of Black girls' history and traditions.

African dance was a place where "shaking the butt" served to connect GEP girls to their African history and thus, removed from the present-day context of hip-hop, created a space to safely explore the sensual and to reclaim their bodies. Ananda, a GEP staff member and professional dancer, addressed these connections between dance, sexuality, and reclaiming oneself through the power of dance. She noted:

> I was in Brazil and I remember my sister talkin' to me about the girls dancing in Senegal and those dances are very much booty and all of

that because that's what they're being introduced to. Yes, "Your body is a sexual instrument as well as a man's." You know, it's not an object for that, but it is definitely an expression of it, as every human being's is. We have to get to a place . . . where we can acknowledge the sexualness of a girl, so that she's not suppressing herself or feeling like she has to then, you know, go the reverse . . . or repress anything like something's wrong with that, you know. And I think that that is—I think that it's that place. I don't know how you get to it, but I think that that has to happen if we really want to see a change. (dance instructor, age thirty-five)

GEP women used African dance as a place to begin the healing, as a place to start the change. They used dance to introduce girls to an alternative lens through which to view not only their past or history but as a way to understand and interpret their present and future.

POPULAR DANCE: GIRLS' ASSERTION OF SELF AND SEXUALITY

THE BEAT

I always dance to the beat.
The beat makes me feel
fly inside and great on the outside.
The beat makes my mind
feel like a buzzing baby.
The beat makes my far-out jeans
fall off of my legs . . .
The beat makes me hot like a tamale.
The beat makes me really hot
with a capital H
with an O
with a capital T (D. Smith, GEP girl)

Dance played an important role within Sun Valley's community as well. It was a critical form of socialization and a prime arena in which to engage in identity work. Rolanda reflected:

GEP girls, group A, gonna dance like that, group B of course they gonna dance like that, group C, I don't know what's they problem, but of course we gonna dance how we want to dance. Ya'll don't live in the part of the city we do. So if ya'll came live where we live, raise your kids up here, you don't think your child is gonna dance exactly like us? We get it from group B and C, we look up to them and Cheryl don't understand that, Ife, and Leslie don't understand that. Yasmine don't understand it. We can't help the way we dance. That is the way we dance around a part where we live, we pick it up from our mommas and when we do the dance, it's not our fault; it's the way we dance. We can't dance like old people, it's not our fault, but we get our dances from going to contests and going against people. We just don't go to ya'll and do all this gymnastics and all of that. (GEP girl, age eleven)

Highlighting the connection between "the part of city" where she lived and the dances that girls would do, Rolanda attached dance, especially popular dance, to the social and cultural context within which it was learned and performed. Therefore, she challenged staff to consider, "If ya'll came live where we live, raise your kids up here, you don't think you child is gonna dance exactly like us?" In many ways, learning and performing particular dances connected GEP girls to the race, class, generational, and gendered realities of Sun Valley and was used to represent their emergent identities.

Research conducted by Kyra Gaunt supports Rolanda's assertions. Gaunt (2006) notes, "In black cultures, dances are acquired as a kind of cultural capital: learned from parents or older siblings, borrowed from dance shows on television and cable" (103). Gaunt suggests that such dances involve Black girls mastering styles of embodiment "that construct their consciousness of themselves as black and female members of a subculture, in contradistinction to the traditions and privilege of the dominant culture, relative to race and gender (among other factors)" (59). As a result, dance can "offer a unique window into the ways we discover and play with our identifications of ourselves as "black," as "black and female," as "American," and as "African" (119).

Clay (2003) found that Black youth use "hip-hop as a form of cultural capital to "keep it real" and authenticate a Black identity as they negotiate peer and neighborhood networks (1351). Clay suggests that Black youth use clothing, posture, speech patterns, and bodily gestures drawn from hip-hop culture to perform their racial identity. For the young women in Clay's study, these performances were tied to the hypersexualized and objectified images of Black females found within hip-hop and especially the music video culture. At issue with each GEP dance performance were questions of authenticity and respect. Specifically, GEP girls drew upon hip-hop dance to solidify their connection to Sun Valley and their race, class, and gender identities as young women from that place. Perfecting and performing the "booty dance" was critical to their claims for authenticity. Tangee noted:

The tootsie roll, the butterfly, and stuff like that . . . young girls do that anyway when they dance, some girls don't do African dances all they life, they like to dance. Like dance to just dance, I don't know. . . they [GEP staff] want them to dance how they dance, they want them to do African dances and stuff. People ain't goin' to like that, they trying to win a prize, like people that is going to attend the talent show ain't goin' to like that. (GEP girl, age sixteen)

For GEP girls, popular dances such as the butterfly and tootsie roll, those you learned in the neighborhood, were a means of getting respect and recognition. In many ways, African dance was not even understood as real dancing—as "dance to just dance." Dance and dance skill, the ability to win the talent show, was based on the ability to dance as defined by local community standards.

Moreover, GEP girls wanted staff to recognize and respect who they were as African American girls from Sun Valley. Kisha, age sixteen, reflected:

You can't tell them what they can do. If this is a community block party, then they part of the community too, you feel me? I know they want us to learn more about African, that kind of dance, but they have to realize that's the kinda' dance we do, they can't take something away that we know. (GEP girl)

At the community talent show, GEP girls actively resisted the staff's control over their bodies and the presentations of their bodies through dance. They wanted staff to respect "something that the girls know"—to respect where they came from. Tangee noted: "They [GEP staff] just want them to be African. Well, they don't want to be African!" (age sixteen). GEP girls wanted staff to recognize that GEP girls were *African American* girls with their own unique culture and values that GEP staff needed to respect. For GEP girls, many of whom adopted a decent working-class femininity, being able to dance reinforced their belonging to Sun Valley. It served to solidify their "racial authenticity." This ability to "keep it real" earned GEP girls respect and served as a form of protection on the streets of Sun Valley.

The discourse of respect has a long tradition within Black communities and has received sociological attention by Elijah Anderson (1999) and Philippe Bourgois (1995). In their ethnographic accounts of the search for respect by youth in the inner cities, they have illustrated that in particular environments, respect, "loosely defined as being treated "right" or being granted one's props (or proper due) or the deference one deserves," is a scarce commodity that oftentimes must literally be fought for and maintained in order to survive (Anderson 1999, 33). While fighting may be the most common strategy to gain respect, respect can also be attained by "getting rec-ognized for achieving a certain standard" (75). For many GEP girls and their female peers, dance, which shapes not only how they are seen but also cre-ates a way for them to manage that seeing, is one avenue to respect. In such community-wide settings, dancing for respect—to win a prize at a commu-nity talent show—involved performing the latest popular dances found within hip-hop culture.

GEP staff's failure to hear or heed the girls' needs and opinions resulted in the multicultural performance. Rolanda remembered:

> The last time we did the thing [multicultural dance performance] they kept on going "Pop" and "Pop," then when we did that dance with Corey and they didn't say nothing about it because our butts weren't at the audience. Once we did our step we had to change three different songs. But the third one didn't have no bad words in it, we didn't even move our butts, we sat on the floor said, "1, 2, 3" and got back up and they acting like that a problem. We had to change our songs four times, change our steps five times. (GEP girl, age eleven)

Similarly, Jamaica recalled:

> We kept havin' to come up with moves where we weren't poppin our booty and stuff . . . and we had to change "Back That Thang Up." Then we had to change that other song where they were talk-ing about girls being nasty with bad words in it. Tonya and Rose started crying, they was like, "Dang, how many more times do we have to change it?" (GEP girl, age eight)

Ten-year-old Mekka recounted:

> Mekka: We did three songs and they told us on that day—it was a Saturday and they told us we couldn't do that off of Destiny's Child and we did it anyway.
> Interviewer: How come you ended up doing it? Did they let you?
> Mekka: No, we just did it.
> Interviewer: So, y'all were like, "We're gonna' do it anyway"?
> Mekka: Yep.
> Interviewer: Whose idea was that?
> Mekka: Ourselves. (GEP girl)

GEP girls resisted staff's organizational and generational authority and used their bodies to present their own decent girl femininity. In reflecting on the event, Rolanda asserted:

> ... the reason why we get mad, because all the time they want us to
> do some African dance, they don't know what we want to do, it
> should be what we want to do, not what they want to do, because
> sometimes what they want to do get a little out of hand. *We can't be
> what GEP wants us to be.* (GEP girl, age eleven)

GEP girls strongly asserted, "We can't be what GEP wants us to be." Speaking with their bodies "should be what we [the girls] wanted to do." As poor and Black, GEP girls were seldom recognized for who they were, but only as what they seemed to be: potential teen mothers, living on welfare. GEP girls used dance to fight for respect. Here, in contrast to a "politics of respectability," in which recognition was based upon an ethos of "as you are like me," girls' "politics of respect" is a push for recognition based upon "seeing me as I am." GEP girls challenged staff to look beyond the stereotyped hypervisibility of poor Black girls' bodies and the invisibility of their personhood.

Hip-hop's sexualized dance moves provided an avenue for girls to challenge GEP staff's control over their bodies. Girls studies scholars have noted that girls' expressions of sexuality can operate as signs of resistance (Bettie 2003). That is, while girls are expected to be feminine, they are also expected to keep overt sexuality hidden, invisible and, most importantly, under control. Sexual explicitness or "sassiness" becomes a way for girls to reject methods of keeping them childlike and to resist both gendered and generational marginalization (McRobbie [1978]1991). For many GEP staff and adults, such sexual displays were direct challenges to the Africentric womanist discourse that identified sexual agency as adult control over the public display of poor Black girls' bodies and sexuality. Girls were aware of and played with staff's reaction. When asked, Kendra summed it up best. She asserted, "I guess that's part of their role. Keep slowing us down" (GEP girl, age eleven). In other words, girls anticipated and even expected GEP's response and understood it as a constant negotiation and testing of limits and power.

Given the racial and gender hierarchy in which GEP girls are embedded, popular dance, with its sexualized repertoire, was a complicated vehicle for identity work. GEP girls moved uneasily between authenticity and their own decent girl respectability. Adams (1999) suggests that many working-class Black girls seek to simultaneously position themselves as "upwardly mobile respectable young women that go to college, enter careers, and achieve success in middle-class society" as well as authentic and "streetwise young women with reputations that afford them the respect they need for survival in the streets and to move beyond the streets into middle-class society" (431). In other words, GEP girls attempted to navigate both authenticity and their decent girl femininity in an effort "to avoid any real losses of family, friends and home identity (Hemmings 2003, 432). While Hemmings focused on girls' use of fighting as a way to secure racial/ethnic authenticity and ultimately respect, I suggest that dance is another such strategy.

GEP girls knew that their dances were provocative. To navigate this tricky terrain girls drew upon a set of unspoken rules. For example, Marlene noted, "We didn't do any freaky dancing . . . like on the floor and stuff and popping my booty in people's faces. The one I did was OK" (GEP girl, age eleven). Alisha chimed in, "Yeah, dropping it and getting back up," that is doing "nasty stuff" (GEP girl, age thirteen). Thus "OK" dances were sassy but not "nasty or freaky." In addition, what moved a dance from sassy to nasty was the intent behind the performance. In response to the girls dancing at the community talent show, Alisha noted that "at least they were smiling, at least they had smiles on their faces, not freakish faces" (GEP girl, age thirteen). These distinctions, while not universally agreed upon within GEP, or even Sun Valley, allowed girls to explore and experiment with the sexualized dance moves and still claim a decent girl femininity.

In the midst of these difficult negotiations and dance politics, girls also experienced pleasure. Popular hip-hop dances provided girls with the space to acknowledge themselves and their emergent sexuality—a space where they could feel "HOT"! McRobbie (1984) suggests that "for women and girls, dance has always offered a channel, albeit a limited one, for bodily self-expression and control; it has also been a source of pleasure and sensuality (133). Yet for many girls dancing was less about sex and more about joyful expression. Ananda noted:

> See the music videos and they see the adult women doin' all that, so they're emulating that. Right? So yeah, we say, "They shouldn't be watching those videos. They shouldn't be doing that." But I think that there's less of a sexual attachment. Like, you know, there are times when I'm dancin' in class and, I'm like being very provocative, but it's not like I'm turned on. I'm just sort of expressing. It's a joyful thing. You know what I mean? And I think with the girls it is, too, but they like—you know, they'll take it to the extreme. You know, "Hah." You get all, you know, down and nasty and it's like, "Yeah." You know they're being defiant. But we get scared because we think, "Oh, my god. They're gonna have sex and they're being sexual," and for the most part what they're doing is they're emulating what they see. (dance instructor, age thirty-five)

Similarly, Gaunt (2006) suggests that dance "highlights an example of 'auto sexuality' " (Miller 1991) in girls' play, where the performance is an expression for themselves, by themselves (84). Dance, especially the sexualized dances performed at the public events, was more about this form of pleasure and mastering styles of movement and gesture to lay claim to an authentic Black identity than erotic or sexual display (Gaunt 2006).

Dance was a key site of struggle within GEP. Girls struggled to present themselves through popular dance, while staff sought to reshape their presentations of young Black femaleness by exercising strict control over the popular dance moves and lyrics. Girls sometimes acquiesced but often resisted. GEP girls' dance routines brought together class and generational conflicts embedded within notions of poor Black girls' sexuality. Girls understood that while staff spoke of sexual agency, they meant sexual control—specifically, adult control over girls' bodies and sexualized expression. Girls fought to be recognized as young adults with their own identities, needs, and desires. It became a generational battle often interpreted through class codes.

This push from the girls caused staff to rethink the suppression of girls' sexuality as well as their own sexuality and began the process of creating openings for girls to express themselves in safe spaces. With regard to girls' dancing, Cheryl, the group B coordinator, noted:

> How I've heard it is that "we know the girls can dance," but that we know that is not all they are capable of doing, so I think that the reason why we've had these conversations is because, we realize it's creative but the messages it's sending about their sexuality, were cautioned. We take caution when putting them out there. I think that it's hard because we spend all this time affirming their talents and gifts and we try to separate it a lot of time from their sexuality, so when they do stuff that is very sexual we kinda put our own stuff in it and say it's negative, because they don't understand the full context of what those thrusts mean in a very sexual way, that they are not aware and so instead of having the conversations, like really talking about the impact of music videos on what we think is cute and how we should carry ourselves, and instead of having those conversations which take a lot of time and deprogramming, we are like, "No, just don't do that." (program coordinator, age twenty-five)

Asha reflected:

> I just had a conversation with one of the girls and we were talking about kissing . . . I was being really honest . . . and just having this really honest dialogue so it's not a secrecy because sexuality should not be this hush-hush thing. So there is that element of honoring sexuality in discussion . . . a really good arena for that to be

expressed is dance, now again I don't think that maybe that should be a public display, but allow them to express that sexual energy. (program coordinator, age twenty-six)

Ananda agreed:

So you know it's not wrong to feel sexual. OK, maybe we gotta do a sexual dance. Maybe we gotta do a dance about what, what is sex to you and what does that mean? And maybe it's not for the public. Maybe it's an exercise just to say, "OK, what was that like?" And let's, you know, let's take the mysticism away from all this and this sort of like closed door, top secret, confidential away and say, "It's normal." It's not wrong to want to sleep with your boyfriend at thirteen or touch him, you know, or your little girlfriend even. So we just have to examine these rules that we've created and say, "OK, yeah. Maybe society says X, Y, Z and it's be goin' on for thousands of years. But let's break this down so at least you know . . . this is an ideology that got set up." It doesn't—most of the time these rules do not reflect what we actually feel, so that doesn't make us wrong, you know. (dance instructor, age thirty-five)

GEP women began the process of having more open conversations about sexuality between themselves and among the girls. They also began to honor popular dance and hired a professional choreographer to teach girls routines that both showcased their talent and "appropriately expressed their sexuality."

In sum, GEP women and girls struggled over the meanings and representations of Black womanhood. This struggle represented an effort to gain control not only over the representations that stereotyped them as loose, licentious, and out of control, but also to exorcise the internal limitations placed upon their own experiences of their bodies. In the process, they emulated, adapted, absorbed, and challenged the prevailing stereotypes and iconography of the Black female dancing body (Gottschild 2003). Although both groups used dance to portray racialized gendered notions of Black femininities, girls used dance to specifically forge class- and age-based femininities and to assert autonomy.

GEP girls fight to be recognized—to be seen outside of the stereotypes that render their bodies hypervisible and their personhood invisible. They assert a desire to be seen, not "as I am like you" but "as I am." They fight to have their voices heard and to experiment and "try on" different ways of being Black and female within a "safe space." From a place of respect, girls push to the foreground the issues of sexuality, metaphorically symbolized and read through dance, so that staff members have had to rethink and come to terms not only with the young women's sexuality but with their own ambivalence regarding their sexuality and desires as Black women. Through the process of empowering themselves, GEP girls have shifted the staff's definition of Black womanhood and have begun the process of making GEP an even safer space.

Conclusion

Imagining Black Womanhood,
Imagining Social Change

I want to be able to have a free life. Some girls must think it is impossible . . . but I want to be able to reach my dreams and go right ahead and follow my goals. (Angela, GEP girl, age twelve)

Where you live don't make you be a different person, it's how you want to picture yourself. (Alisha, GEP girl, age thirteen)

I imagined this would be a really safe space to just be myself, and just be really valued and affirmed. (Cheryl, program coordinator, age twenty-five)

Robin Kelley, in his book *Freedom Dreams*, suggests that our collective imagination may be the most revolutionary power available to us. Specifically, he writes "our imagination can enable us to imagine a new society, imagine something different, to realize that things need not always be this way" (Kelley 2002, 9). I titled this book *Imagining Black Womanhood* in an effort to highlight the powerful role of the imagination in Black women's and girls' identity work. Specifically, I wanted to emphasize the capacity of Black women's and girls' imaginations to "convert the given confines of here and now into an open horizon of possibilities" (Kearney 1998, 2) and to highlight the places where real girls must make sense of who they are in the midst of conflicting and often contradictory images and discourses of Black womanhood. I wanted to illustrate their desire and ability to dream their way to individual and collective freedom.

Organizations such as GEP, while imperfect, are critical to the construction and maintenance of such dreams. They provide opportunities for youth

145

to "reframe and re-imagine not only the type of world in which we choose to live but also to reframe and re-imagine who we want to be in [the] world" (Ginwright 2008, 14). Through their work together, GEP women and girls created a space where they could step outside of dominant frames and representations of Black womanhood to construct nurturing bonds across lines of difference and imagine and articulate critical, albeit contradictory, race-class-gender discourses. GEP served as a site of empowerment.

Audre Lorde, however, cautions against one-sided celebratory tales of Black women's support, connection, and empowerment and reminds us that Black women's spaces of safety also can be fraught with tension. She writes:

> Often we give lip service to the idea of mutual support and connection between Black women because we have not yet crossed the barriers to these possibilities, nor fully explored the angers and fears that keep us from realizing the power of a real Black sisterhood. . . . We have not been allowed to experience each other freely as Black women in America; we come to each other coated in myths, stereotypes, and expectations from the outside, definitions not our own. (1984, 153)

GEP was not an exception. Here Black women and girls had to imagine and negotiate who they were within the context of dominant and internalized representations that stereotyped them as sexually aggressive, deviant, and out of control—stereotypes that fostered the creation of GEP as a pregnancy prevention program and staff's attempts to control GEP girls. In addition, GEP women and girls had to negotiate their class and generational differences and, consequently, power differences. The results of this negotiation had intended and unintended consequences that created opportunities for empowerment as well as experiences of increased marginalization. These contradictory results speak to the perfect imperfection of homeplaces.

In this case study, I explored the "fragile and tenuous" nature of safe spaces in which groups come together to imagine and construct images of self across lines of difference. My claim that organizational context is critical in identity work has been borne out by evidence of GEP's organizational power matrix reproducing and disrupting Black women's and girls' location within limiting discursive and power fields. I have attempted to move beyond essentialist arguments that suggest that race-gender sameness automatically creates spaces of empowerment. Instead, I have shown that Black women's and girls' identity work is about both empowerment and marginalization, shaped and structured not only by larger macro-structural forces but also by the organizational context within which their identity work occurs.

I found that while GEP was constructed as a space for girls' empowerment, both women and girls made use of the organization to resist dominant representations of Black womanhood and construct alternative and resisting Black femininities. Both women and girls empowered themselves. For GEP women, empowerment took the form of developing a program grounded in an Africentric womanist understanding, with and against the mandates of the founders. That is, GEP women shifted the organization's mission statement from a deficit-based model built upon the images of Black women as welfare queens and jezebels, read through the stereotype of "The Urban Girl," to a program grounded in Africentric womanist youth development committed to "enabling Black girls to access their power." Thus Black females were represented as "Strong Girls" and "Powerful Women." This was a significant shift that reorganized how both power and empowerment were conceptualized, and how power moved within the organization.

As part of this reconfiguration, GEP women built upon their personal experiences as well as GEP's organizational discourse and practice to construct a discourse of Africentric womanist femininity along three dimensions: (1) self-definition, (2) self-reliance, and (3) sexual agency. This version of Black womanhood, while clearly embedded within and in conversation with larger discourses, was not a case of Black women attempting to emulate or mimic middle-class White womanhood. Moreover, it also was not an attempt to strengthen and support the indigenous myth of strong Black womanhood. Instead, it was an attempt to create a model in which Black women could critique dominant and indigenous images, such as welfare queen, superwoman, "skezzer," and "golddigger," and to redefine themselves. Thus GEP women produced a vision of Black womanhood not by simply adopting external ideologies but through a very creative, challenging process in which they created their own ideologies and frameworks.

For GEP girls, empowerment took the form of articulating their own decent girl femininity with and against the mandates of GEP staff, dominant discourses of "The Urban Girl," and local community conceptions of "ghetto." Specifically, GEP girls articulated a working-class Black femininity that also emphasized the goal of self-determination and characteristics of self-definition, self-reliance, and sexual agency. Rather than being understood as antagonistic to GEP's discourses and practices, girls' understanding of Black womanhood mapped onto GEP's discourse. Girls chose to participate in the GEP because of the program's celebration of an independent Black womanhood and its emphasis on education as a vehicle for upward social mobility. As a result, rather than challenging the central tenets of Africentric womanism, GEP girls challenged GEP to live up to its stated claims—to allow *all* Black women to self-determine, specifically with regard to heterosexual displays of Black women's sexuality. Thus despite its contra-dictory race-class-gender-sexuality ideologies, GEP, in practice, served as an arena for empowerment—its core mission from the beginning.

In addition, I found that Black women and girls used two different strategies to negotiate their visions of Black womanhood: for the women, a "politics of respectability"; for the girls, a "politics of respect." GEP women's articulation of Africentric womanist femininity contained a tension between authenticity and respectability: "Be yourself" versus "Be like us"; "Move your body however you want" versus "Don't dance like a ho"; "Own your body" versus "Don't get pregnant." Thus despite the goal of self-determination and self-definition for all Black women, GEP women constructed a hierarchy of Black femininities whereby Africentric womanism, embodied in the public persona of Lauryn Hill, came to represent the model of femininity to which all others became subordinated. Key to their "politics of respectability" was an attempt to destabilize the hypersexualized representations of Black wom-anhood that had justified and normalized Black women's and girls' exploita-tion and marginalization. Moreover, they attempted to police and silence the expression of other forms of femininities, in an effort to "protect" GEP girls *and* themselves from increased surveillance, further sexual exploitation, and the denial of opportunities.

In contrast, GEP girls utilized a politics of respect to challenge the Afri-centric womanist femininity promoted and practiced within GEP. In particu-lar, GEP girls fought to be recognized—to be seen outside of the stereotypes that rendered their bodies hypervisible and their personhood invisible. They asserted a desire to be seen, not "as I am like you" but "as I am." They fought to have their voices heard and to experiment and "try on" different ways of being Black and female within a "safe space." From a place of respect, girls pushed to the fore the issues of sexuality, metaphorically symbolized and read through dance, such that staff had to rethink and come to terms with not only the young women's sexuality—most often expressed through dance—but their own ambivalence regarding their sexuality and desires as Black women. Through the process of empowering themselves, GEP girls shifted the staff's definition of Black womanhood and continued the process of making GEP an even safer space.

The struggles over identity explored within GEP remind us that identi-ties and identity work do not happen "out there" but often within organiza-tions that have their own logics and processes. In this work I proposed the term *organizational power matrix* to address the theoretical shortcomings found within research on identity work. Here organizational culture, struc-ture, and environment are conceptualized as ideological, positional, and material domains of power that intersect and interact to create an organiza-tional power matrix that confers and denies power. In this way, these domains serve as resources that organizational actors mobilize in pursuit of their goals and, in this case, identity work, the construction of a safe space, and empowerment.

Within GEP, the organizational power matrix disrupted everyday social relations with the effect of creating a space in which both Black women and girls were able to empower themselves. Specifically, GEP women mobilized the cultural and positional power available to them through the organization's structure and Africentric womanism discourses. GEP girls, on the other hand, mobilized their organizational power gained via the organization's youth power discourse and their status as consumers rather than clients within the organization. Consequently, power moved through GEP in ways and with results that the founders and even administrators did not anticipate.

This study provides a conceptual analysis of the relationship between identity work and organizational context. Its qualitative nature provides both advantages and limitations. Qualitative methods have allowed me to explore the hidden transcripts and processes of identity work negotiation, often masked in historical and macro-level studies. However, inherent in qualitative research is the partial and oftentimes incomplete picture captured by the researcher's own angle of vision and position in society. Moreover, given the case study design of the project, more field-based and comparative research is needed to examine the interaction between organizational context and identity work across various settings. For example, I had the opportunity to interview women from several girl-serving organizations in the Bay Area. Of particular note was a program run by Black women for Black girls living in a public housing development neighboring Sun Valley. Several questions became immediately apparent: Given that this organization did not have an explicitly Africentric womanist framework, how would power and empowerment be conceptualized within this space? How would Black womanhood be imagined, defined, resisted, and negotiated?

LAST WORDS

In sum, GEP served as a contradictory site of empowerment and resistance whereby Black women and girls created a "fragile and tenuous" space in which to construct alternative Black femininities as well as to develop and refine a critical race and gender consciousness. Ananda reflected:

> We can unlearn all of the things that we've learned that have been so detrimental to us as Black women, as women of color, and share that with each other. . . . Bein' able to come together and have

forums where we can get to the dirty stuff. You know what I mean? And we need mediators and people to, you know, keep us in check so we don't take out stuff on each other. But that forum to me is just as crucial, because if you don't get to that there's a whole lot of stuff that doesn't get said, and there's a whole lot of stuff of like what it means to be politically correct. And when you don't feel politically correct, you don't feel safe to be able to express what you know. It's like jealousy is not politically correct. Hatred, self-hatred and hatred of others who reflect you is not politically correct, so you're not gonna admit to it. But it's gonna come out, and it's gonna come out in ways of like, "Well, you didn't clean the kitchen" or "You didn't do this."

But being able to have forum for us as women and for girls where we're able to just be safe. You know what I mean? And that's hard, really hard to create those safe spaces and . . . we have to teach the girls. And that even if we're just learning it, we've got to teach them. But that takes me being in that learning process. So it's not about having it figured out. The only way that we can really, really pass the ideas that we want for them is by the fact that we're working on it. And if we think we have it down, that's a problem, that's a problem. *If you think you know it, that's a problem. If you know you're learning it, that's where it's at.* (dance instructor, age thirty-five, emphasis added)

For Ananda, the construction of a safe place is an ongoing process of learning: "If you think you know it, that's a problem. . . . If you know you're learning it, that's where it's at." The creation of such a space must therefore be understood as constantly under construction, waxing and waning with the learning processes of both women and girls. Throughout this process, margins and the center will shift, and understanding the ways organizations can center and marginalize becomes an important part of the growth process. But a safe space alone cannot transform the public sphere—this is only a starting point, not an end unto itself.

Appendix

Interview Guide

Background

1. How old are you?
2. What grade are you in?
3. What is your racial identity?
4. With whom do you live?
5. How would you describe your family?
6. Where do you live?
7. How long have you lived there?
8. How would you describe the neighborhood in which you grew up?
9. How long have you attended GEP?

Family

1. Whose idea was it for you to attend GEP?
2. What is your relationship like with your parents/caregivers and siblings?
3. Do you talk with your parents/caregivers about GEP? If so, what about?
4. What do you think your parents would like for you to be learning at GEP?
5. Have there been any conflicts between your parents and GEP? If so, what were they?

Inside GEP

1. What is your favorite activity/program at GEP?
2. Do you feel that what you are learning at GEP is relevant to your life?
3. How do you feel about GEP staff?
4. If you could plan activities for GEP for a week, what would you do?
5. What contributions do you feel you make to GEP?
6. How have things changed since you have been here?
7. If you could change anything at GEP, what would you change?
8. Have you changed since attending GEP? If so, how?
9. How would you describe the girls who attend GEP?
10. What would a "successful GEP girl" look like? Act like?
11. What would a "GEP failure" look like? Act like?
12. How would you describe the relationships between the girls within GEP?
13. Does GEP have any effect on how you feel about being a Black girl?
14. What do your friends think about GEP?
15. Do you have friends that don't attend GEP? Why not?
16. What do the men/boys in your life think about GEP?
17. How do you feel about attending an all-girls program?
18. What do you like best about GEP being all girls? The least? Do you wish GEP admitted boys?

Gender Relations

1. What is it like being a girl today?
2. When does a girl become a woman? What are some of the qualities/ characteristics that separate a girl from a woman?
3. Do you consider yourself a girl or a woman?
4. Are there things you would like to see changed about relationships between men and women?
5. Who are your role models? Or are there women you would like to be like when you grow up?
6. Are there women you do not want to be like?

Race Relations

1. How is life different or the same for you as a girl of color?
2. Would you want GEP to admit White girls into the program? Other girls of color? Why/Why not?

Hot Spots (Power, Teen Pregnancy, and Dance)

1. What do you see yourself doing ten years from now? Who and what influenced your decision?
2. What do you think about girls who become mothers as teens?
3. What generally happens when GEP girls become pregnant?
4. What do you think GEP should do when girls get pregnant?
5. What happened when the little girls started dancing at the community talent show?
6. Do you think it was okay for them to dance like that?
7. What happens when GEP girls dance?

GEP STAFF AND BOARD OF DIRECTORS

Background

1. Tell me a little about yourself.
2. How old are you?
3. What is your racial identity?
4. How would you describe your family?
5. Where do you live?
6. How long have you lived there?
7. How would you describe the neighborhood in which you grew up?
8. In which social class do you locate yourself?
9. When did you begin working at GEP? What circumstances brought you to teach here?
10. Describe a healthy Black woman.
11. What are some of the challenges facing young Black girls today?
12. How do you attempt to help girls overcome these challenges?
13. What are some of the similarities and differences between when you were growing up and now?

Inside GEP

1. How would you describe GEP?
2. How has the experience of teaching inside a single-sex, African-centered program been for you? Has it had any impact on your teaching?
3. Have you heard of the terms *Africentric* and *womanist*? If so, where did you first hear those terms? What do they mean to you? Do you think

GEP is Africentric and womanist? In what sense? How do you see Africentric womanism operating within GEP? Do you consider yourself Afrocentric and womanist? If you worked for another organization that was not Afrocentric and womanist, how might your work be different?

4. What are your goals as a program coordinator, executive director, board member?
5. Has the experience of working at GEP changed over the years? If so, in which ways? To what do you attribute the changes?
6. How have you changed since you've been working at GEP?
7. How do you define success in working at GEP? Is there anything that prevents you from being as successful as you would like to be? How would you describe a successful GEP girl?
8. Is there anything that you especially like or dislike about working at GEP or would like to see changed?
9. How would you describe your relationship with the administration?
10. How do you see power operating within GEP?
11. Do you consider your work at GEP political?
12. Would you like to change careers in the future? To what, and why?
13. What are the biggest conflicts between GEP girls and staff? Between staff and parents?

Hot Spots (Power, Teen Pregnancy, and Dance)

1. What do you think about girls who become mothers as teens?
2. What generally happens when GEP girls become pregnant?
3. What do you think GEP should do when girls get pregnant?
4. What happened when the little girls started dancing at the community talent show?
5. Do you think it was okay for them to dance like that?
6. What happens when GEP girls dance?
7. What is the role of African dance inside GEP?

PARENTS

Background

1. Tell me a little about yourself.
2. How old are you?
3. What is your racial identity?
4. How would you describe your family?

5. Where do you live?
6. How long have you lived there?
7. How would you describe the neighborhood in which you grew up?
8. Describe a healthy Black woman.
9. What are some of the challenges facing young Black girls today?
10. How do you attempt to help girls overcome these challenges?
11. What are some of the similarities and differences between when you were growing up?

Inside GEP

1. How did you learn about GEP? Why did you choose to send your daughter here?
2. Could anything have prevented you from sending her there? If your child did not attend GEP, then where would she go after school?
3. How would you characterize the educational experience at GEP?
4. What would you like your daughter to learn while she is here?
5. What kinds of women do you feel GEP is interested in trying to create?
6. Has your daughter changed during the time she has attended GEP? If so, in what way?
7. What are some of your daughter's goals? What do you think of them? Does GEP encourage your daughter to pursue these goals?
8. What would you like to see your daughter's life like after she graduates from high school?
9. How would you describe a successful Black woman?
10. What are your feelings about teen motherhood?
11. In what ways do you think your daughter's life will be the same or different from yours? Do you feel GEP plays a role in influencing her life in these directions?
12. How do you feel about the staff at GEP? What kind of influence do you feel they have had on your daughter and her future?
13. What would you like to see changed at GEP?
14. Are you involved with GEP in any way? If so, how? What role do you feel parents play in the GEP community? To what extent is this role encouraged or discouraged by GEP? Are you involved at your daughter's school?
15. Have there been any conflicts between you and GEP?
16. If you had to do it all over again, would you send your daughter to GEP?
17. What do you see as the role for a young woman in 2000?
18. What are some of the qualities/characteristics that separate a girl from a woman?

19. Have you heard of the terms *Afrocentric* and *womanist?* Is so, where did you first hear those terms? What do they mean to you? Do you think GEP is Afrocentric and womanist? In what sense? Do you consider yourself Africentric and womanist?
20. Are there things you would like to see changed about relationships between men and women? About women's and men's roles?
21. Are there women you do not want your daughter to be like?

Hot Spots (Power, Teen Pregnancy, and Dance)

1. What do you see yourself doing ten years from now? Who and what influenced your decision?
2. What generally happens when GEP girls become pregnant?
3. What do you think GEP should do when girls get pregnant?
4. What happened when the little girls started dancing at the community talent show?
5. Do you think it was okay for them to dance like that?
6. What happens when GEP girls dance?
7. What do you see as the role of African dance within GEP?

Notes

INTRODUCTION

1. All names of persons, places, and organizations have been changed.
2. Throughout the book, I reproduce participants' responses, both verbal and written, in their original form. As a result, I have chosen not to use [sic] when non-standard English is used.
3. GEP uses the word "Africentric" rather than the word "Afrocentric." The rationale is that "Afri" comes directly from the word Africa, while "Afro" attempts to emulate "Euro" from Europe.
4. The quoted comments are taken from a video clip of the April 4 edition of MSNBC's "Imus in the Morning," found at Media Matters for America, http://www.mediamatters.org/items/200704040011. This is not the first time Don Imus has been at the center of racial controversy.
5. This two-day event was aired on April 16–17, 2007. Day one, entitled: "After Imus, Now What?," featured prominent Black leaders. Day two, titled "After Imus, the Hip-Hop Community Responds," featured Russell Simmons, Common, and other hip-hop artists.
6. In the wake of the Imus controversy, renewed interest sprung up around the representations of Black women in our collective imagination. Two documentaries, The *Souls of Black Girls* and A *Girl Like Me*, capture the impact of media representations on Black girls' self-image and identity. Both films make visible the ways existing stereotypes shape and constrain not only how others perceive Black women and girls but also how African American women and girls construct a self-identity. To emphasize this point, Daphne Valerius, the writer, editor, and producer of *The Souls of Black Girls*, asserts that Black girls "suffer internally from a triple consciousness condition, having to be a Negro, an American and a woman within our society (Valerius 2008). She suggests that Black girls may be suffering from a "self-image disorder" as a result of trying to attain the standards of beauty celebrated within popular culture.

157

7. Emerson (2002) suggests that "the racialized nature of the sexist expectations of femininity create a paradox, a contradiction for young Black girls" (89). Locked out and "derided for being inherently inferior to white women," she asserts that their position as outsiders may afford them some "protection" against the dominant scripts of silence, passivity, and obedience (90). This is not to suggest that all Black girls are liberated from these norms but, rather, to consider that they may be less constrained by the particular messages associated with this form of femininity.

8. "I Can't Make You Love Hannah If You Don't," season 1, episode 4 (originally aired April 14, 2006; watched on ABC Kids, June 2008).

9. From Hannah Montana recap on tv.com: http://www.tv.com/hannah-montana/i-cant-make-you-love-hannah-if-you-dont/episode/620807/recap.html, accessed 7-23-08.

10. From Hannah Montana recap on tv.com: http://www.tv.com/hannah-montana/i-cant-make-you-love-hannah-if-you-dont/episode/620807/recap.html, accessed 7-23-08.

11. Researchers have found that even when controlling for socioeconomic status, African American children and teens consistently consume more media than all other groups (Whites and other racial ethnic groups) (Blosser 1988; Greenberg 1993). Hansen and Hansen (2000) found that 60.7 percent of videos on BET were found to contain sexual content, compared to 23 percent of videos on MTV. The sexual scripts in Black music, especially hip-hop and R&B videos, reinforce stereotypical images of Black women and men as hypersexual, amoral, and materialistic (Emerson 2002).

12. For example, in his study of Mobilization for Youth (MFY), a nonprofit program focusing on juvenile delinquency and poverty, Helfgot ([1974]1981) argued that despite the organization's explicit structural theory about the nature of poverty, a culture of poverty ideology soon pervaded its programs as a result of the organization's elite sponsors. That is, MFY's funders exerted normative pressure on MFY, which subsequently reproduced this rhetoric in an effort to acquire funds. It shifted the official organizational culture and consequently the ideological frameworks and resources available to members.

CHAPTER 1

1. Ninety percent of the girls were African American, and 10 percent were Pacific Islander and/or multiracial. Over the course of any given year, 45 percent of the girls participated in a full year of programming, while 20

percent remained for one to three months and 35 percent dropped in sporadically or for support during a crisis. Finally, almost 30 percent of the girls participated in the program for three years or more (GEP 1998).

2. Many residents of Sun Valley and outsiders alike assume that Sun Valley was former military housing due to the barrack-type housing and arrangement of units.

3. Information based upon interviews with residents found in a GEP evaluation report by Elaine Peacock (1999).

4. According to the Sentencing Project, between 1986 and 1991 the number of Black women in state prisons on drug-related charges alone soared a staggering 828 percent (Mauer and Huling 1995). The majority of women imprisoned for crack were Black. Women were sentenced for five, ten, or fifteen years for possession of crack cocaine. As a result, Black children were nine times more likely to have an incarcerated parent than White children (Krisberg and Temin 2001). They represented 43 percent of all children of incarcerated mothers.

5. For an extended treatment of such relationships, see Stack 1997.

CHAPTER 2

1. In the early decades of the twentieth century, with the rise of the urban industrial centers in the North, thousands of African Americans left the rural South and moved into Northern cities to escape sharecropping and the lynch mob. The United States was in a period of postwar economic boom, and factory work represented a chance to achieve the "American dream" for many low-skilled and poorly educated African Americans. Low-skilled here refers to little experience or training in the industrial or professional labor market sectors. Many of the migrants were highly skilled in the agricultural sector. However, these skills were of little value in the urban labor market.

2. By the mid-1970s, the United States, facing increased "international competition, declining productivity and output in key domestic manufacturing sectors, low rates of capital investment, and rising cost (particularly after the oil shock of 1974), was beset by deep and persistent economic troubles" (Wolch 1990, 38). The most pressing was stagflation, or "simultaneous inflation and low gross national product growth" (Wolch 1990, 38). As a result of stagflation, the unemployment rate soared, poverty expanded, and families sought out government assistance in the form of unemployment and Aid to Families with Dependent Children (AFDC) in record numbers (Wilson 1987; Wolch 1990).

3. In general, the mother's pension was never intended for poor Black women. Rather, it was created to support widowed White mothers so they could tend to their "work" of raising a productive White citizenry. Black women, on the other hand, were repeatedly denied claim to grants-in-aid if any fieldwork was available, or if they had been employed as seasonal day laborers. (For an extensive treatment of Black women's exclusion from the mother's pension, see Sheared 1998; Amott 1990.)

4. Blacks' welfare utilization has varied substantially from 1930 to the present and can be divided into three periods. The first period, from the late 1930s to the 1960s, can be characterized as exclusionary. Welfare utilization during this period was sharply restricted due to the exclusion of industries heavily populated by Blacks from eligibility and overt discriminatory practices. The second period, from the 1960s to the mid-1970s, was a time of Black women asserting their entitlement to welfare. At this time, many of the discriminating restrictions were struck down, and Black women's participation in the welfare program rose dramatically. The third period, from the mid-1970s until today, can be characterized as diminishing access and contested entitlement (Amott 1990, 287).

5. For an in-depth explanation of public and private patriarchy, see Ferree 1995.

6. They fought for restrictive birth control and abortion legislation that required parental consent as a condition of service (see Hyde 1995; Luker 1996; Roberts 1997). The use of public money, including Medicaid funds, to pay for abortions was prohibited in 1980 in Harris v. McRae; in Webster v. Reproductive Health Services in 1989, the Supreme Court ruled that states could impose a range of restrictions on abortions (Perlmutter 1994, 160). In addition to increasing legal and political opposition, anti-choice forces mounted protests and demonstrations at many women's health facilities.

7. In other words, while the Reagan administration took the lead on the dismantling of the welfare state, this process has continued despite party affiliation of presidential leadership. The Personal Responsibility and Work Opportunity Act, considered a major victory of the Clinton administration, made major changes in the U.S. welfare system. The primary goal of this act was to shift the emphasis from long-term financial support to short-term, time-limited financial assistance, predicated upon the active movement of the families' heads of households into the workforce. The act replaced AFDC with Temporary Assistance for Needy Families (TANF) and established work participation requirements (workfare) for receiving TANF benefits. It also instituted a five-year benefit limit to TANF recipients.

8. Kaplan (1997) notes that for working-class mothers, the class aspirers, their daughter's pregnancy represented a lost opportunity for their own class mobility. On the other hand, middle-class mothers of teen moms interpreted their daughter's pregnancy as a loss in class status—a slide back into the working class.

9. The videotaped beating of Rodney King took place in 1991 and the acquittal of the four LAPD officers in 1992.

10. *Community foundations* are nonprofit, tax-exempt, grant-making organizations. These foundations are public charities, since they develop broad support from many unrelated donors with a wide range of charitable interests in a specific community. A community foundation has an independent board that is broadly representative of the public interest, and it maintains a diverse grants program that is not limited in scope. *Independent foundations* are nongovernmental, nonprofit organizations with funds (usually from a single source, such as an individual, a family or a corporation) and programs managed by its own trustees or directors, established to maintain or aid social, educational, religious, or other charitable activities serving the common welfare, primarily through grant-making to other nonprofit organizations. A private foundation does not solicit funds from the public.

11. Personal correspondence.

12. For a case study where this was not so, see Sheridan-Rabideau 2008.

13. Foundations included the following: San Francisco Foundation, James Irvine Foundation, Women's Foundation, Family Friedman Fund, Tides Foundation, Stuart Foundation, Koret Foundation, Walter Johnson Foundation, Mckesson Corporation, and Heller Foundation.

14. To grasp the size difference, consider that in 2003 the Friedman Family Foundation granted approximately $1 million, whereas the SF Foundation granted over $68 million.

15. Stuart Foundation home page, accessed 7-8-2003.

16. Freidman Family Fund home page, accessed 7-9-2003.

17. GEP still had difficulty generating start-up funding. It was considered an "expensive" or a "cadillac" program with a high-average-dollar allotment per girl. In addition, the tenant empowerment component was considered very risky.

CHAPTER 3

1. For a critique of Wilson's work, see Reed 1999.

2. Afrocentricity places Africa at the center of any analysis of African American experience and was developed as a corrective to the

Eurocentic paradigm that places European civilization, history, and experience not only at the center of philosophical, psychological, and even biological analysis but also deems that experience as universal. For a cogent critique of Afrocentricity, see Gilroy 1993b.

3. See Statistical Record of Black America 1995, tables 346, 347.

4. As a way to measure the extent of girls' loss of voice and self, the American Association of University Women (AAUW) (1992) conducted a national survey on gender and self-esteem. As part of this project, over 3,000 boys and girls between the ages of nine and fifteen were polled on their attitudes toward self, school, family, and friends. Based on their findings, the researchers charged that instead of providing girls with opportunities and encouraging intellectual growth, public schools were failing girls. Both boys and girls in the survey reported widespread gender bias in the classroom. Respondents reported that boys got more attention in the classroom and were encouraged to be more assertive, and that girls were not encouraged to pursue science and math.

5. For more detail on the controversy, see AAUW 1998. See also Salomone 2005.

6. Kwanzaa is an African American celebration of family, community, and self determination created by Maulana Karenga in 1966. Today Kwanzaa is celebrated from December 26 to January 1 by more than 18 million people worldwide (see http://www.tike.com/celeb-kw.htm, accessed June 5, 2009).

7. The Nguzo Saba are the seven guiding principles of Kwanzaa. They are Umoja (Unity), Kujichagulia (Self-Determination), Ujima (Collective Work and Responsibility), Ujamaa (Cooperative Economics), Nia (Purpose), Kuumba (Creativity), and Imani (Faith).

8. Afrocentric scholars are rightly criticized because their conceptualization of culture relies on the notion of an African "essence" (hooks and West 1992). This is not to argue that "Africanisms" did not survive the Middle Passage and slavery but, rather, to suggest that the "significance and meaning of these survivals has been irrevocably sundered from their origins" (Gilroy 1993a, 223).

9. From participant observation and interview notes from an employee orientation training.

CHAPTER 4

1. Feminist scholars and activists argued that "form could not be divorced from the content" (Rothschild 1976, 28) and pushed for the creation of collective organizations (Evans 1979; Freeman 1974; O'Sullivan 1976).

Collectives were ideal organizations that provided not only an alternative but also a direct contrast to the bureaucratic organizational structure. Whereas bureaucracies emphasized hierarchical relations and power as domination and control, collectives were based upon the principles of feminism and emphasized participatory decision making; rotating leadership; power conceptualized as empowerment; and social relations based on personal, communal, and holistic ideals (Rothschild-Whitt 1979; Bordt 1997).

2. See Bordt 1997; Gottfried and Weiss 1994; Iannello 1992; Leidner 1991; Reinelt 1995.

3. Americorp provides full-time members to community organizations to create and expand programs that aim to build capacity and ultimately bring low-income individuals and communities out of poverty (see http://www.americorps.org/, accessed 1-7-2009. Writers Corp places professional writers in community settings to teach creative writing to youth (see http://www.sfartscommission.org/WC/, accessed 1-7-2009. GEP relied upon both of these organizations to provide programs for the girls.

4. I draw upon the work of feminist and, in particular, intersectional theories of power employing the metaphor of the matrix to examine women's and girls' resistance. From this perspective, varying axes of power, such as race, class, gender, age, and sexuality, work with and against each other in a nonhierarchical fashion, producing intersecting and overlapping relations of power that vary across historical, cultural, institutional, and organizational contexts (Collins 1991; hooks 1981; Cohen 1999; Raby 2006). Due to the intersection of such axes, we exist in what can be shifting positions of dominance and subordination and are often simultaneously agents and "victims" of power (Foucault 1983). Within this framework, domination is not hegemonic.

5. Delta Sigma Theta Sorority, Inc., is a private, non-profit organization whose purpose is to provide assistance and support through established programs in local communities throughout the world. (See http://www.deltasigmatheta.org/cms/, accessed 12-18-2008.)

CHAPTER 5

1. This separation of hip-hop into distinct generations is not without controversy. While not a formal study, I did note differences between the teens, twenty-somethings, and thirty-somethings with regard to ideas about sexuality and their relationship to hip-hop. All participants felt they were members of the hip-hop generation, and yet they had a very

different meaning for each group and spoke to qualitatively different lived experiences and, consequently, hip-hop experiences.

2. See Miller 2008.
3. See Watts 2002.
4. See Hill 1998.

CHAPTER 6

1. For a detailed discussion of the significance of the "butt" in the White imagination, see Gilman 1985. In his article he describes the European fascination with the buttocks and the linking of "big butts" with hypersexuality and deviance. His work links the depictions of European prostitutes with Sarah Bartmann and the construction of not only Black women's sexuality but also Black sexuality as a whole.
2. It seems that the elementary-age girls enjoyed African dance. Group B girls, consistent with middle school pressures, only wanted to perform hip-hop dance. And group C girls, much more aware of the objectification and sexualization of their bodies, refused to dance at all.

Works Cited

Acker, Joan. 1994. "Feminist Goals and Organizing Processes." In *Feminist Organizations: Harvest of the New Women's Movement*, ed. M. M. Ferree and P. Y. Martin, 137–44. Philadelphia, PA: Temple University Press.

Adams, Natalie G. 1999. "Fighting to Be Somebody: Resisting Erasure and the Discursive Practices of Female Adolescent Fighting." *Educational Studies* 30(2):115–39.

Alan Guttmacher Institute. 1994. *Sex and the American Teenager*. New York: AGI.

Allen, Theodore W. 1975. "They Would Have Destroyed Me: Slavery and the Origins of Racism." *Radical America* 9: 41–63.

Alvesson, Mats, and Yvonne D. Billing. 1997. *Understanding Gender and Organizations*. London: Sage Publications.

American Association of University Women (AAUW). 1992. *How Schools Shortchange Girls: A Study of the Major Findings on Girls and Education*. Wellesley College, MA: Center for Research on Women.

———. 1998. *Separated by Sex: A Critical Look at Single Sex Education for Girls*. Washington, DC: AAUW Educational Foundation.

Amott, Teresa. 1990. "Black Women and AFDC: Making Entitlement out of Necessity." In *Women, the State and Welfare*, ed. L. Gordon, 280–300. Madison: University of Wisconsin Press.

Anderson, Elijah. 1990. *Streetwise: Race, Class, and Change in an Urban Community*. Chicago, IL: University of Chicago Press.

———. 1999. *Code of the Street: Decency, Violence and the Moral Life of the Inner City*. New York: W.W. Norton and Company.

Anyon, Jean. 1983. "Intersections of Gender and Class: Accommodation and Resistance by Working-Class and Affluent Females to Contradictory Sex-Role Ideologies." In *Gender, Class, and Education*, ed. S. Walker and L. Barton, 19–38. London: Falmer Press.

Arnot, Madeline. 1982. "Male Hegemony, Social Class and Women's Education." *Journal of Education* 164: 64–89.

Asante, Molefi K. 1988. *Afrocentricity*. Trenton, NJ: Africa World Press.

———. 1990. *Kemet, Afrocentricity and Knowledge*. Trenton, NJ: Africa World Press.

Ascher, Carol. 1991. *School Programs for African American Male Students*. New York: ERIC Clearinghouse on Urban Education.

Baldwin, Davarian. 2004. "Black Empires, White Desires: The Spatial Politics of Identity in the Age of Hip-Hop." In *That's the Joint!: The Hip-Hop Studies Reader*, ed. M. Forman and M. A. Neal, 159–76. New York: Routledge.

Barnett, Bernice McNair. 1995. "Black Women's Collectivist Movement Organizations: Their Struggles during the 'Doldrums'." In *Feminist Organizations: Harvest of the New Women's Movement*, ed. M. M. Ferree and P. Y. Martin, 199–222. Philadelphia, PA: Temple University Press.

Barth, Fredrik. 1969. *Ethnic Groups and Boundaries*. Boston, MA: Little, Brown & Co.

Bartle, Elizabeth, Graciela Couchonnal, Edward Canda, and Martha Stake. 2002. "Empowerment as a Dynamically Developing Concept for Practice." *Social Work* 47(1): 32–44.

Beauboeuf-Lafontant, Tamara. 2005. "Keeping Up Appearances, Getting Fed Up: The Embodiment of Strength among African American Women." *Meridians: Feminism, Race, Transnationalism* 5(2):104–23.

Belenky, Mary, Blythe Clinchy, Nancy Goldberger, and Jill Tarule. 1986. *Women's Ways of Knowing*. New York: Basic Books.

Bennett, Claudette E. 1995. "The Black Population in the United States: March 1994 and 1993." U.S. Bureau of the Census, *Current Population Reports*, series P20-480. Washington, DC: U.S. Government Printing Office.

Best, Amy. 2000. *Prom Night: Youth Schooling and Popular Culture*. New York: Routledge.

Bettie, Julie. 2003. *Women without Class: Girls, Race and Identity*. Berkeley: University of California Press.

Bey-Cheng, Laina, and Amanda Lewis. 2006. "Our 'Ideal Girl': Prescriptions of Female Adolescent Sexuality in a Feminist Mentorship Program." *Afflia* 21: 71–83.

Beyer, Janice. 1981. "Ideologies, Values and Decision Making in Organizations" In *Handbook of Organizational Design*, vol. 2, ed. P. Nystrom and W. H. Starbuck, 162–202. New York: Oxford University Press.

Blosser, B. J. 1988. "Ethnic Differences in Children's Media Use." *Journal of Broadcasting & Electronic Media* 32: 453–70.

Bordt, Rebecca. 1997. *The Structure of Women's Nonprofit Organizations.* Bloomington: Indiana University Press.

Bourdieu, Pierre. 1984. *Distinction: A Social Critique of the Judgment of Taste.* Cambridge, MA: Harvard University Press.

Bourgois, Philippe. 1995. *In Search of Respect: Selling Crack in El Barrio.* New York: Cambridge University Press.

Bowles, Samuel, and Herbert Gintis. 1976. *Schooling in Capitalist America: Educational Reform and the Contradictions of Economic Life.* New York: Beacon Books.

Brown, Lyn Mikel. 1998. *Raising Their Voices: The Politics of Girls' Anger.* Cambridge, MA: Harvard University Press.

Brown, Lyn Mikel, and Carol Gilligan. 1990. *Meeting at the Crossroads: Women's Psychology and Girls' Development.* Cambridge, MA: Harvard University Press.

Browne, Karen. 1976. "Reassessing Basics." *Quest: A Feminist Quarterly* 2(3): 31–37.

Calhoun, Craig. 1994. "Social Theory and the Politics of Identity." In *Social Theory and the Politics of Identity*, ed. C. Calhoun, 9–36. Cambridge, MA: Blackwell.

Campbell, Anne. 1984. *The Girls in the Gang: A Report from New York City.* Oxford: Basil and Blackwell.

Carby, Hazel. 1987. *Reconstructing Womanhood: The Emergence of the Afro-American Women Novelist.* New York: Oxford.

———. 1997. "Policing the Black Woman's Body in an Urban Context." In *Women Transforming Politics*, ed. C. Cohen, K. Jones, and J. Tronto, 151-66. New York: New York University Press.

Clark, Verna, and Associates. 1996. "GEP Program Evaluation Report." Evaluation Report Submitted to the Girls Empowerment Project. Unpublished report.

Clay, Andreanna. 2003. "Keepin' It Real: Black Youth, Hip-Hop Culture, and Black Identity." *American Behavioral Scientist* 46(10): 1346–58.

Cohen, Cathy. 1996. "Contested Membership: Black Gay Identity and the Politics of AIDS." In *Queer Theory Sociology*, ed. S. Seidman, 362–94. Oxford: Blackwell.

———. 1999. *The Boundaries of Blackness: AIDS and the Breakdown of Black Politics.* Chicago, IL: University of Chicago Press.

Collins, Patricia Hill. 1991. *Black Feminist Thought: Knowledge, Consciousness, and the Politics of Empowerment.* New York: Routledge.

———. 1998. *Fighting Words: Black Women and the Search for Justice.* Minneapolis: University of Minnesota Press.

———. 2004. *Black Sexual Politics.* New York: Routledge.

Connell, R.W. 1987. *Gender and Power.* Stanford, CA: Stanford University Press.

Cowie, C., and S. Lees. 1981. "Slags or Drags." *Feminist Review* 9: 17–31.

Craig, Maxine Leeds. 2002. *Ain't I a Beauty Queen?: Black Women, Beauty & the Politics of Race.* New York: Oxford University Press.

Crenshaw, Kimberle. 1992. "Whose Story Is It Anyway? Feminist and Anti-Racists Appropriations of Anita Hill." In *Race-ing Justice, En-gendering Power*, ed. T. Morrison, 402–40. New York: Pantheon Books.

Davis, Angela. 1981. *Women, Race and Class.* London: The Women's Press.

———. 1998. *Blues Legacies and Black Feminism: Gertrude "Ma" Rainey, Bessie Smith, and Billie Holiday.* New York: Pantheon.

Davis, Lynn. 1983. "Gender, Resistance and Power." In *Gender, Class, and Education*, ed. S. Walker and L. Barton, 39–52. London: Falmer Press.

Deem, Rosemary. 1983. "Gender, Patriarchy, and Class in the Popular Education of Women." In *Gender, Class, and Education*, ed. S. Walker and L. Barton, 107–22. London: Falmer Press.

DeFrantz, Thomas. 2002. *Dancing Many Drums: Excavations in African American Dance.* Madison: University of Wisconsin Press

Dill, Bonnie Thorton. 1979. "The Dialectics of Black Womanhood." *Signs* 4: 543–55.

DiMaggio, Paul. 1982. "Cultural Entrepreneurship in Nineteenth-Century Boston: The Creation of an Organizational Base for High Culture in America." *Media, Culture, and Society* 4: 33–50.

DiMaggio, Paul, and Walter Powell. 1991[1983]. "The Iron Cage Revisited: Institutional Isomorphism and Collective Rationality." In *The New Institutionalism in Organizational Analysis*, ed. W. Powell and P. DiMaggio, 63–82. Chicago, IL: University of Chicago Press.

Dugger, Celia. 1992. "H.I.V. Incidence Rises among Black Mothers: Infection Rate Drops for White Mothers." *New York Times*, May 1, B3.

Eisenhart, Margaret, and Dorothy Holland. 1983. "Learning Gender from Peers: The Roles of Peer Groups in the Cultural Transmission of Gender." *Human Organization* 42: 321–32.

———. 1990. *Educated in Romance: Woman, Achievement, and College Culture.* Chicago, IL: University of Chicago Press.

Emerson, Rana. 2002. "African American Teenage Girls and the Construction of Black Womanhood in Mass Media and Popular Culture." *African American Research Perspectives* 8(1): 85–102.

Evans, Sara. 1979. *Personal Politics: The Roots of the Women's Liberation Movement in the Civil Rights Movement and the New Left.* New York: Random House.

Evans, Sara M., and Harry C. Boyte. 1986. *Free Spaces: The Sources of Democratic Change in America.* New York: Harper and Row.

Ferguson, Ann. 2000. *Bad Boys: Public School in the Making of Black Masculinity*. Ann Arbor: University of Michigan Press.

Ferguson. Kathy. 1984. *The Feminist Case against Bureaucracy*. Philadelphia, PA: Temple University Press.

———. 1987. "Male-Ordered Politics: Feminism and Political Science." In *Idioms of Inquiry: Critique and Renewal in Political Science*, ed. T. Ball, 209–30. Albany: State University of New York Press.

Ferree, Myra Marx. 1995. "Patriarchies and Feminisms: The Two Women's Movements of Post-Unification Germany." *Social Politics* 2: 10.

Fields, Barbara. 1990. "Slavery, Race and Ideology in the United States of America." *New Left Review* 18 (May/June): 95–118.

Finch, Lynette. 1993. *The Classing Gaze: Sexuality, Class and Surveillance*. St. Leonard's, NSW, Australia: Allen & Unwin.

Fine, Michelle, and Nancie Zane. 1995. "Bein' Wrapped Too Tight: When Low-Income Women Drop Out of High School." In *Dropouts from School: Issues, Dilemmas, and Solutions*, ed. L.Weis, E. Farrar, and H. Petrie, 23–54. Albany: State University of New York Press.

Fisher, Sue, and Kathy Davis, eds. 1993. *Negotiating at the Margins: The Gendered Discourses of Power and Resistance*. New Brunswick, NJ: Rutgers University Press.

Flax, Jane. 1990. *Thinking Fragments: Psychoanalysis, Feminism and Post-Modernism in the Contemporary West*. Berkeley: University of California Press.

Fordham, Signithia. 1993. " 'Those Loud Black Girls' ": Black Women, Silence, and Gender 'Passing' in the Academy." *Anthropology and Education Quarterly* 24: 3–32.

———. 1996. *Blacked Out: Dilemmas of Race, Identity, and Success at Capital High*. Chicago, IL: University of Chicago Press.

Foucault, Michel. 1978. *The History of Sexuality: Volume 1*. New York: Vintage Books.

———. 1980. *Power/Knowledge*. New York: Pantheon.

———. 1984. *The Foucault Reader*. Edited by P. Rabinow. New York: Pantheon Books.

Frankenberg, Ruth. 1993. *White Women, Race Matters: The Social Construction of Whiteness*. Minneapolis: University of Minnesota Press.

Freeman, Jo. 1974. "The Tyranny of Structurelessness." In *Women in Politics*, ed. J. Jacquette, 202–14. New York: John Wiley and Sons.

Freiberg, P. 1991. "Separate Classes for Black Males?" *APA Monitor* (May) 1: 47.

Fried, Amy. 1994. " 'It's Hard to Change What We Want to Change': Rape Crisis Centers as Organizations." *Gender & Society* 8(4): 562–83.

Friedman Family Foundation. 1992. *Annual Report*.

Fuller, Mary. 1980. "Black Girls in a London Comprehensive School." In *Schooling for Women's Work*, ed. R. Deem, 52–65. London: Routledge & Kegan Paul.

Galper, Jeffery H. 1975. *The Politics of Social Service*. Englewood Cliffs, NJ: Prentice Hall.

Gamble, Dinese, and Associates. 1999. "GEP Evaluation Report." *Final Report Submitted to the Girls Empowerment Project*. Unpublished report.

Gamson, Joshua. 1996. "The Organizational Shaping of Collective Identity: The Case of Lesbian and Gay Film Festivals in New York." *Sociological Forum* 11: 231–59.

Gaunt, Kyra. 2006. *The Games Black Girls Play: Learning the Ropes from Double-Dutch to Hip-Hop*. New York: New York University Press.

GEP (Girls Empowerment Project). 1992a. "All about GEP." Overview of Program Sent to Potential Funders. Unpublished document.

———. 1992b. "Girls Empowerment Project: For Inner-City Mothers of Tomorrow." Funding Proposal Submitted to Potential Funders. Unpublished document.

———. 1992c. "Memo to Executive Committee." Memo Submitted to GEP Executive Committee. Unpublished document.

———. 1993. "A Progress Report." Memo Submitted to GEP Executive Committee. Unpublished document.

———. 1998. "A Funding Proposal." Request for Funds Submitted to Various Foundations. Unpublished document.

Giddings, Paula. 1984. *When and Where I Enter: The Impact of Black Women on Race and Sex in America*. New York: William Morrow and Company.

Gilman, Sander. 1985. "Black Bodies, White Bodies: Toward an Iconography of Female Sexuality in Late Nineteenth-Century Art, Medicine, and Literature." *Critical Inquiry* 12(1): 205–43.

Gilroy, Paul. 1987. *There Ain't No Black in the Union Jack*. London: Hutchinson.

———. 1993a. *Black Atlantic*. Cambridge, MA: Harvard University Press.

———. 1993b. *Small Acts: Thoughts on the Politics of Black Cultures*. London: Serpent's Tail.

Ginwright, Shawn. 1999. "Identity For Sale: The Use of Racial and Cultural Identity in Urban School Reform." *Urban Review* (32): 87–104.

———. 2002. "Classed Out: The Challenges of Social Class in Black Community Change." *Social Problems* 49(4): 544–62.

———. 2008. "Collective Radical Imagination: Youth Participatory Action Research and the Art of Emancipatory Knowledge." In *Revolutionizing Education: Youth Participatory Action Research in Motion*, ed. J. Cammarota and M. Fine, 13–22. New York: Routledge.

Glenn, Evelyn Nakano. 1992. "From Servitude to Service Work: Historical Continuities in the Racial Division of Paid Reproductive Labor." *Signs: Journal of Women in Culture and Society* 18(1): 1–43.

Gottfried, Heidi, and Penny Weiss. 1994. "A Compound Feminist Organization: Purdue University's Council on the Status of Women." *Women in Politics* 14(2): 23–44.

Gottschild, Brenda. 2003. *The Black Dancing Body: A Geography from Coon to Cool.* New York: Palgrave Macmillan.

Gramsci, Antonio. 1971. *Selections from the Prison Notebooks of Antonio Gramsci.* Edited and translated by Q. Hoare and G. N. Smith. New York: International Publishers.

Greenberg, B. 1993. "Race Differences in TV and Movie Behaviors." In *Media, Sex, and the Adolescent*, ed. B. Greenberg, J. Brown, and N. Buerkel-Rothfuss, 145–52. Creskill, NJ: Hampton.

Gregg, Nina. 1993. " 'Trying to Put First Things First': Negotiating Subjectivities in a Workplace Organizing Campaign." In *Negotiating at the Margins: The Gendered Discourses of Power and Resistance*, ed. S. Fisher and K. Davis, 172–204. New Brunswick, NJ: Rutgers University Press.

Griffin, Christine. 1985. *Typical Girls? Young Women from Schools to the Job Market.* London: Routledge and Kegan Paul.

Guerra, Becky. 1997. "GEP Surveys: A Compilation of Responses and Suggestions for Future Evaluation." Survey Results Submitted to the Girls Empowerment Project. Unpublished document.

Hall, Richard. 1987. *Organizations: Structures, Processes and Outcomes.* Englewood Cliffs, NJ: Prentice Hall.

Hall, Stuart. 1973. *Encoding and Decoding in Television Discourse.* Birmingham, England: Center for Cultural Studies, University of Birmingham.

———. 1990. "Cultural Identity and Diaspora." In *Identity: Community, Culture, Difference*, ed. J. Rutherford, 222–37. London: Lawrence and Wishart.

———. 1996 [1986]. "Gramsci's Relevance to the Study of Race and Ethnicity." In *Stuart Hall: Critical Dialogues in Cultural Studies*, ed. D. Morley and K-H. Chen, 411–41. New York: Routledge.

———. 1997. "Subjects in History: Making Diasporic Identities." In *The House that Race Built*, ed. W. Lubiano, 289–300. New York: Pantheon Books.

Hall, Stuart, and Tony Jefferson. 1976. *Resistance through Rituals: Youth Cultures in Post-War Britain.* London: Hutchinson.

Haney, Lynne. 1996. "Homeboys and Men in Suits: The State and the Reproduction of Male Dominance." *American Sociological Review* 61: 759–78.

Hansen, C. H., and R. Hansen. 2000. "Music and Music Videos." In *Media Entertainment: The Psychology of Its Appeal*, ed. D. Zillmann and P. Vorderer, 175–96. Mahwah, NJ: Lawrence Erlbaum.

Harder, P., J. Musselwhite Jr., and Lester Salamon. 1984. *Government Spending in the Nonprofit Sector in San Francisco*. Washington, DC: The Urban Institute Press.

Harder, P., M. Kimmich, and Lester Salamon. 1985. *The San Francisco Bay Area Nonprofit Sector in a Time of Government Retrenchment*. Washington, DC: The Urban Institute Press.

Harding, Sandra. 1987. "Introduction: Is There a Feminist Method?" In *Feminism and Methodology: Social Science Issues*, ed. S. Harding, 1–14. Bloomington: Indiana University Press.

———. 1991.*Whose Science? Whose Knowledge?* Ithaca, NY: Cornell University Press.

Health, Shirley B., and Milbrey W. McLaughlin, eds. 1993. *Identity and Inner-City Youth: Beyond Ethnicity and Gender*. New York: Teachers College Press.

Hebdige, D. 1979. *Subcultures: The Meaning of Style*. London: Methuen.

Helfgot, Joseph. [1974]1981. *Professional Reforming: Mobilization for Youth and the Failure of Social Science*. Lexington, MA: Lexington Books.

Hemmings, Annette. 2003. "Fighting for Respect in Urban High Schools." *Teachers College Record* 105(3): 416–37.

Higginbotham, Evelyn Brooks. 1992. "African American Women's History and the Metalanguage of Race." *Signs: Journal of Women in Culture and Society* 17: 251–74.

———. 1993. *Righteous Discontent: The Women's Movement in the Black Baptist Church, 1880–1920*. Cambridge, MA: Harvard University Press.

Hill, Lauryn. 1998. "Every Ghetto, Every City" *The Mis-education of Lauryn Hill*. Columbia Records.

Holland, Dorothy, and Madeline Eisenhart. 1981. "Women's Peer Groups and Choice of Career." Final Report for the National Institute of Education. Washington, DC: ERICED.

hooks, bell. 1981. *Ain't I a Woman: Black Women and Feminism*. Boston, MA: South End Press.

———. 1989. *Talking Back: Thinking Feminist, Thinking Black*. Boston, MA: South End Press.

———. 1990. *Yearning: Race, Gender, and Cultural Politics*. Boston, MA: South End Press.

———. 1992. *Black Looks: Race and Representation*. Boston, MA: South End Press.

hooks, bell, and Cornell West. 1992. *Breaking Bread: Insurgent Black Intellectual Life*. Boston, MA: South End Press.

Hudson, Barbara. 1984. "Femininity and Adolescence." In *Gender and Generation*, ed. A. McRobbie and M. Nava, 31–53. London: Macmillan.

Hyde, Cheryl. 1995. "Feminist Social Movement Organizations Survive the New Right." In *Feminist Organizations: Harvest of the New Women's Movement*, ed. M. Ferree and P. Martin, 306–22. Philadelphia, PA: Temple University Press.

Iannello, Kathleen. 1992. *Decisions without Hierarchy: Feminist Interventions in Organizational Theory and Practice*. New York: Routledge.

Interaction Associates. 1997. *Facilitative Leadership: Tapping the Power of Participation*. San Francisco, CA: Interaction Associates LLC.

Irvine, Janice. 1994. *Sexual Identities and the Construction of Adolescent Identities*. Philadelphia, PA: Temple University Press.

James Irvine Foundation. 1992. *Annual Report*.

Johnson, J., M. Adams, L. Ashburn, and W. Reed. 1995. "Differential Gender Effects of Exposure to Rap Music on Black Adolescents' Acceptance of Teen Dating Violence." *Sex Roles* 33: 597–605.

Kanter, Rosabeth Moss. 1998. "The Impact of Hierarchical Structures on the Work Behavior of Women and Men." In *Feminist Foundations: Towards Transforming Society*, ed. K. Meyers, C. Anderson, and B. Risman, 259–77. London: Sage Publications.

Kaplan, Elaine Bell. 1997. *Not Our Kind of Girl: Unraveling the Myths of Black Teenage Motherhood*. Berkeley: University of California Press.

Katzenstein, Mary Fainsod. 1990. "Feminism within American Institutions: Unobtrusive Mobilization in the 1980s." *Signs* 16(1): 27–54.

Kearney, Richard. 1998. *The Wake of the Imagination*. New York: Routledge.

Kelley, Robin. 2002. *Freedom Dreams: The Black Political Imagination*. Boston, MA: Beacon Press.

King, Deborah. 1995. "Multiple Jeopardy, Multiple Consciousness: The Context of Black Feminist Identity." In *Words of Fire*, ed. B. Guy-Sheftall, 293–318. New York: The New Press.

Kornegger, Peggy. 1975. "Anarchism: The Feminist Connection." *The Second Wave* 4: 36–37.

Krisberg, Barry, and Carolyn Temin. 2001. *The Plight of Children Whose Parents Are in Prison*. NCCD Focus. Oakland, CA: National Council on Crime and Delinquency.

Kunjufu, Jawanza. 1985. *Countering the Conspiracy to Destroy Black Boys*. Chicago, IL: African American Images.

Ladner, Joyce. 1972. *Tomorrow's Tomorrow: The Black Woman*. Garden City, NY: Doubleday.

Lamont, Michele. 1989. "The Power-Culture Link in a Comparative Perspective." *Comparative Social Research* 11: 131–50.

Leadbeater, Bonnie, and Niobe Way. 1996. *Urban Girls: Resisting Stereotypes, Creating Identities*. New York: New York University Press.

Lees, Sue. 1986. *Losing Out: Sexuality and Adolescent Girls*. London: Hutchinson.

Leidner, Robin. 1991. "Stretching the Boundaries of Liberalism: Democratic Innovation in a Feminist Organization." *Signs* 16(2): 263–89.

Levinson, Bradley, and Dorothy Holland. 1996. "The Cultural Production of the Educated Person: An Introduction." In *The Cultural Production of the Educated Person*, ed. B. Levinson, D. Foley, and D. Holland, 1–56. Albany: State University of New York Press.

Lord, Robert, and Karen Maher. 1991. *Leadership and Information Processing: Linking Perceptions, Organizational Culture and Performance*. Boston, MA: Unwin Hyman.

Lorde, Audre. 1984. *Sister Outsider: Essays and Speeches*. Berkeley, CA: Crossing Press.

Lubiano, Wahneema. 1992. "Black Ladies, Welfare Queens, and State Minstrels: Ideological War by Narrative Means." In *Race-ing Justice, Engendering Power*, ed. T. Morrison, 323–63. New York: Pantheon Books.

Luker, Kristin. 1996. *Dubious Conceptions: The Politics of Teenage Pregnancy*. Cambridge, MA: Harvard University Press.

Luttrell, Wendy. 1989. "Working-Class Women's Ways of Knowing: Effects of Gender, Race, and Class." *Sociology of Education* 62: 33–46.

———. 1997. *School-Smart and Mother-Wise: Working Class Women's Identity and Schooling*. New York: Routledge.

Mansbridge, Jane. 1984. "Feminism and the Forms of Freedom." In *Critical Studies in Organization and Bureaucracy*, ed. F. Fischer and C. Sirianni, 544–53. Philadelphia, PA: Temple University Press.

Martin Patricia Yancey. 1990. "Rethinking Feminist Organizations." *Gender and Society* 4(2): 182–206.

Mauer, Marc, and Tracy Huling. 1995. *Young Black Americans and the Criminal Justice System: Five Years Later*. Washington, DC: The Sentencing Project.

McCormick, Erin. 2001. "Census Showing Black Population Plummeting in Last Decade in S.F." *San Francisco Chronicle*, June 17, A1, A2.

McLaughlin, Milbry, Merita Irby, and Juliet Langman. 1994. *Urban Sanctuaries: Neighborhood Organizations in the Lives and Futures of Inner City Youth*. San Francisco, CA: Jossey-Bass.

McRobbie, Angela. [1978]1991. "Girls and Subcultures." In *Feminism and Youth Culture: From "Jackie" to "Just Seventeen,"* ed. A. McRobbie, 12–25. London: Macmillan.

———. 1984. "Dance and Social Fantasy." In *Gender and Generation*, ed. A. McRobbie and M. Nava, 130–61. London: Macmillan.

MEE (Motivational Educational Entertainment). 2005. *This Is My Reality—The Price of Sex: An Inside Look at Black Urban Youth Sexuality and the Role of the Media*. Washington, DC: National Campaign to Prevent Teen Pregnancy.

Miller, Dan. 1991. "*Asolute Freedom in Trinidad.*" *Man* 26(June): 323–341.

Miller, Jody 2008. *Getting Played: African American Girls, Urban Inequality and Gendered Violence*. New York: New York University Press.

Mills, Terry, Craig Bolystein, and Sandra Lorean. 2001. " 'Doing' Organizational Culture in the Saturn Corporation." *Organization Studies* 22(1): 117–43.

Milofsky, Carl. 1987. "Neighborhood-Based Organizations: A Market Analogy." In *The Non-Profit Sector: A Research Handbook*, ed. W. Powell, 277–95. New Haven, CT: Yale University Press.

Milofsky, Carl, and Frank Romo. 1988. "The Structure of Funding Arenas for Neighborhood Based Organizations." In *Community Organizations: Studies in Resource Mobilization and Exchange*, ed. C. Milofsky, 177–242. New York: Oxford University Press.

Moi, Toril. 1991. "Appropriating Bourdieu: Feminist Theory and Pierre Bourdieu's Sociology of Culture." *New Literary History* 22(4): 1019–49.

Morgan, Joan. 1999. *When Chickenheads Come Home to Roost: A Hip-Hop Feminist Breaks It Down*. New York: Touchstone.

Morgen, Sandra. 1994. "Personalizing Personnel Decisions in Feminist Organizational Theory and Practice." *Human Relations* 47(6): 665–84.

Morken, Kristin, and Per Selle. 1994. "The Women's Shelter Movement." In *Women and Social Change: Non-Profits and Social Policy*, ed. F. Perlmutter, 133–57. Washington, DC: National Association of Social Workers.

Musselwhite, James Jr., L. Salamon, P. Harder, and P. Holcomb. 1987. *Human Services Spending in San Francisco County: The Changing Roles of Government and Private Funders*. Washington, DC: The Urban Institute Press.

Myllyluoma, Jaana, and Lester Salamon. 1992. *The San Francisco Bay Area Nonprofit Sector: An Update*. Baltimore, MD: Johns Hopkins University Press.

Narine, Marcia. 1992. *Single-Sex, Single-Race Public Schools: A Solution to the Problems Plaguing the Black Community?* Washington, DC: U.S. Department of Education.

Nava, Mica. 1984. "Youth Service Provision, Social Order and the Question of Girls." In *Gender and Generation*, ed. A. McRobbie and M. Nava, 1–30. London: Macmillan.

Navarro, Mireya. 1992. "Left Behind by AIDS: A Parent Dies and a Teen-Ager Aches." *New York Times*, May 6, B1, B2.

Nettleford, Rex. 1998. "Foreword." In *African Dance: An Artistic, Historical and Philosophical Inquiry*, ed. K. Asante, xiii–1. Trenton, NJ: Africa World Press.

Nielsen, Waldemar. 1995. *The Golden Donors: A New Anatomy of the Great Foundations*. New York: Dutton Press.

Omalade, Barbara. 1995. "Hearts of Darkness." In *Words of Fire: An Anthology of African American Feminist Thought*, ed. B. Guy-Sheftall, 361–78. New York: The New Press.

Omi, Michael, and Howard Winant. 1994. *Racial Formation in the United States: From the 1960s to the 1990s*. New York: Routledge.

O'Neale, Sondra. 1986. "Inhibiting Midwives, Usurping Creators: The Struggling Emergence of Black Women in American Fiction." In *Feminist Studies/Critical Studies*, ed. T. de Lauretis, 139–56. Bloomington: Indiana University Press.

O'Neil, Michael. 1989. *The Third America: The Emergence of the Nonprofit Sector in the United States*. San Francisco, CA: Jossey-Bass.

Ostrander, Susan A. 1999. "Gender and Race in a Pro-Feminist, Progressive, Mixed-Gender, Mixed-Race Organization." *Gender and Society* 13: 628–42.

O'Sullivan, Liz. 1976. "Organizing for Impact." *Quest* 2(3): 68–80.

Painter, Nell. 1992. "Hill, Thomas, and the Use of Racial Stereotypes." In *Racing Justice, Engendering Power*, ed. T. Morrison, 200–14. New York: Pantheon.

Pardo, Mary. 1995. "Doing It for the Kids: Mexican American Community Activists, Border Feminist?" In *Feminist Organizations: Harvest of the New Women's Movement*, ed. M. Ferree and P. Martin, 356–71. Philadelphia, PA: Temple University Press.

Pastor, Jennifer, Jennifer McCormick, and Michelle Fine. 1996. "Makin' Homes: An Urban Girl Thing." In *Urban Girls: Resisting Stereotypes, Creating Identities*, ed. B. Leadbeater and N. Way, 15–34. New York: New York University Press.

Peacock, Elaine. 1999. *GEP Meta Analysis*. Final Report Submitted to the Girls Empowerment Project. Unpublished report.

Perlmutter, Felice. 1994. *Women and Social Change: Non-Profits and Social Policy*. Washington, DC: National Association of Social Workers.

Pipher, Mary. 1994. *Reviving Ophelia: Saving the Selves of Adolescent Girls*. New York: Ballantine Books.

Pittman, Karen, Raymond O'Brien, and Mary Kimball. 1993. *Youth Development and Resiliency Research: Making Connections to Substance Abuse Prevention*. Commissioned Paper #9. Oakbrook, IL: Midwest Center for Drug-Free Schools and Communities.

Polhemus, Ted. 1993. "Dance, Gender and Culture." In *Dance, Gender and Culture*, ed. H. Thomas, 3–16. New York: St. Martin's Press.

Ponse, Barbara. 1978. *Identities in the Lesbian World: The Social Construction of Self*. Westport, CT: Greenwood Press.

Poster, Winifred R. 1995. "The Challenges and Promises of Class and Racial Diversity in the Women's Movement: A Study of Two Women's Organizations." *Gender and Society* 9: 659–79.

Powell, Walter. 1987. *The Non-Profit Sector: A Research Handbook*. New Haven, CT: Yale University Press.

Powell, Walter, and Rebecca Friedkin. 1987. "Organizational Change in Non-Profit Organizations." In *The Non-Profit Sector: A Research Handbook*, ed. W. Powell, 180–94. New Haven, CT: Yale University Press.

Primus, Pearl 1994 [1998]. "African Dance." In *African Dance: An Artistic, Historical, and Philosophical Inquiry*, ed. K. Asante, 3–12. Trenton NJ: African World Press.

Raby, Rebecca. 2006. "Talking (Behind Your) Back: Girls and Resistance." In *Girlhood: Redefining the Limits*, ed. Yasmin Jiwani, Claudia Mitchell, and Candis Steenbergen, 138–54. Montreal: Black Rose Books.

Reed, Adolph. 1999. *Stirrings in the Jug: Black Politics in the Post-Segregation Era*. Minneapolis: University of Minnesota Press.

Reinelt, Claire. 1995. "Moving into the Terrain of the State: The Battered Women's Movement and the Politics of Engagement." In *Feminists Organization Harvest of the New Women's Movement*, ed. M. Ferree and P. Martin, 84–104. Philadelphia, PA: Temple University Press.

Reinharz, Shulamit. 1992. *Feminist Methods in Social Research*. New York: Oxford University Press.

Roberts, Dorothy. 1997. *Killing the Black Body: Race, Reproduction and the Meaning of Liberty*. New York: Pantheon Books.

Robinson, Tracy, and Janie Ward. 1991. "'A Belief in Self Far Greater than Anyone's Disbelief': Cultivating Healthy Resistance among African American Female Adolescents." In *Women, Girls, and Psychotherapy: Reframing Resistance*, ed. C. Gilligan, A. G. Rogers, and D. L. Tolman, 87–104. Binghamton, NY: Harrington Park Press.

Rothschild, Joan. 1976. "Taking Our Future Seriously." *Quest* 2(3): 17–30.

Rothschild-Whitt, Joyce. 1979. "The Collectivist Organization: An Alternative to Rational-Bureaucratic Models." *American Sociological Review* 44: 509–27.

Sadker, Myra, and David Sadker. 1994. *Failing at Fairness: How America's Schools Cheat Girls*. New York: Scribner Book Company.

Salamon, Lester. 1995. *Partners in Public Service: Government and Nonprofit Relations in the Modern Welfare State.* Baltimore, MD: Johns Hopkins University Press.

Salem, Dorothy. 1990. *To Better Our World: Black Women in Organized Reform, 1890–1920.* Brooklyn, NY: Carlson.

Salomone, Rosemary. 2005. *Same, Different, Equal: Rethinking Single Sex Schooling.* New Haven, CT: Yale University Press.

San Francisco Foundation. 1992. *Annual Report.*

Sassen, Saskia. 1994. *Cities in a World Economy.* Thousand Oaks, CA: Pine Forge Press.

Schilt, Kirsten. 2003. "'I'll Resist with Every Inch and Every Breath': Girls and Zine Making as a Form of Resistance." *Youth and Society* 35(1): 71–97.

Schippers, Mimi. 2004. "Femininity, Masculinity and Gender Hegemony." Paper presented at the Annual Meeting of the American Sociological Association, Hilton San Francisco & Renaissance Parc 55 Hotel, San Francisco, CA. Online. http://www.allacademic.com/meta/p110250_index.html.

Scott, James. 1990. *Domination and the Arts of Resistance: Hidden Transcripts.* New Haven, CT: Yale University Press.

SFDSS. 1992. *Department of Social Services Report.* Unpublished report.

SFHA. 1992. *Housing Authority Report.* Unpublished report.

———. 1998. *Housing Authority Report.* Unpublished report.

———. 2007. *Housing Authority Report.* Unpublished report.

Sharpley-Whiting, T. 2007. *Pimps Up Ho's Down: Hip-Hop's Hold on Young Black Women.* New York: New York University Press.

Sheared, Vanessa. 1998. *Race, Gender and Welfare Reform: The Elusive Quest for Self-Determination.* New York: Garland.

Sheridan-Rabideau, Mary P. 2008. *Girls, Feminism, and Grassroots Literacies: Activism in the Girl Zone.* Albany: State University of New York Press.

Skeggs, Beverley. 1997. *Formations of Class and Gender: Becoming Respectable.* London: Sage.

Smith, Dorothy. 1987. *The Everyday World as Problematic: A Feminist Sociology.* Boston, MA: Northeastern University Press.

Snow, David, and Leon Anderson. 1987. "Identity Work among the Homeless: The Verbal Construction and Avowal of Personal Identities." *American Journal of Sociology* 92: 1336–71.

Spelman, Elizabeth V. 1988. *Inessential Woman: Problems of Exclusion in Feminist Thought.* Boston, MA: Beacon Press.

Stack, Carol. 1997. *All Our Kin: Strategies for Survival in a Black Community.* New York: Bantam Books.

Stake, Robert. 1995. *The Art of Case Study Research.* Thousand Oaks, CA: Sage Publications.

Stall, Susan, and Randy Stoecker. 1998. " 'Community Organizing or Organizing Community': Gender and the Crafts of Empowerment." *Gender and Society* 12(6): 729–56.

Statistical Record of Black America. 1995. Detroit, MI: Gale Research.

Stevens, Joyce. 2002. *Smart and Sassy: The Strengths of Inner-City Black Girls.* New York: Oxford University Press.

Strouse, Jeremiah, Megan Goodwin, and Bruce Roscoe. 1994. "Correlates of Attitudes toward Sexual Harassment among Early Adolescents." *Sex Roles* 31: 559–77.

Sudbury, Julia. 1998. *"Other Kinds of Dreams": Black Women's Organisations and the Politics of Transformation.* London: Routledge.

Tayeb, Monir. 1988. *Organizations and National Culture: A Comparative Analysis.* London: Sage.

Terrelonge, Pauline. 1995. "Feminist Consciousness and Black Women." In *Words of Fire: An Anthology of African American Feminist Thought,* ed. B. Guy-Sheftall, 489–502. New York: The New Press.

Thomas, Helen, ed. 1993. *Dance, Gender and Culture.* New York: St. Martin's Press.

Tolman, Deborah L. 1996. "Adolescent Girls' Sexuality: Debunking the Myth of the Urban Girl." In *Urban Girls: Resisting Stereotypes, Creating Identities,* ed. B. Leadbeater and N. Way, 255–71. New York: New York University.

Trinh, Minh-Ha. 1991. *When the Moon Waxes Red: Representation, Gender, and Culture Politics.* New York: Routledge.

Valerius, Daphne S. 2008. "The Souls of Black Girls." DVD. Directed, produced, and narrated by Daphne S. Valerius. Los Angeles: Femme Noir Productions.

Wagner, Venise. 1998. "Learning How to Be Themselves" *S.F. Chronicle,* October 25, D1, D4.

Waldinger, Roger. 1996. *Still the Promised City? African Americans and New Immigrants in Postindustrial New York.* Cambridge, MA: Harvard University Press.

Walker, Alice. 1983. *In Search of Our Mothers' Gardens.* New York: Harcourt Brace Jovanovich.

Wallace, Michelle. 1994. *Invisibility Blues: From Pop to Theory.* New York: Verso.

Ward, Janie V. 1990. "Racial Identity Formation and Transformation." In *Making Connections: The Relational World of Adolescent Girls at Emma Willard School,* ed. C. Gilligan, N. P. Lyons, and T. J. Hanmer, 215–32. Cambridge, MA: Harvard University Press.

Ward, Janie V., and Beth Benjamin. 2004. "Women, Girls and the Unfinished Work of Connection: A Critical Review of American Girls

Studies." In *All about the Girl: Culture, Power and Identity*, ed. A. Harris, 15–28. New York: Routledge.

Ward, Monique L., Edwina Hansbrough, and Eboni Walker. 2005. "Contributions of Music Video Exposure to Black Adolescents' Gender and Sexual Schemas." *Journal of Adolescent Research* 20(2): 143–66.

Ward, Monique L. 2002. "Does Television Exposure Affect Emerging Adults' Attitudes and Assumptions about Sexual Relationships? Correlational and Experimental Confirmation." *Journal of Youth and Adolescence* 31: 1–15.

Watts, Eric King. 2002. "The Female Voice in Hip-Hop: An Exploration into the Potential of the Erotic Appeal." In *Centering Ourselves: African American Feminist and Womanist Studies of Discourse*, ed. M. Houston and O. Davis, 187–213. Cresskill, NJ: Hampton Press.

Weber, Nathan. 1991. *Independent Youth Development Organizations: An Exploratory Study*. Washington, DC: Carnegie Council on Adolescent Development.

White, Deborah Gray. 1999. *Too Heavy a Load*. New York: W.W. Norton and Company.

White, Frances E. 2001. *Dark Continent of Our Bodies: Black Feminism and the Politics of Respectability*. Philadelphia, PA: Temple University Press.

Willis, Paul. 1977. *Learning to Labor: How Working-Class Kids Get Working-Class Jobs*. New York: Columbia University Press.

Wilson, William J. 1987. *The Truly Disadvantaged: The Inner City, the Underclass, and Public Policy*. Chicago, IL: University of Chicago Press.

Wolch, Jennifer. 1990. *The Shadow State: Government and Voluntary Sector in Transition*. New York: The Foundation Center.

Women's Building. 1992. *Annual Report*.

Woodson, Carter G. [1933]1972. *The Mis-Education of the Negro*. New York: AMS Press.

Ylvisaker, Paul. 1987. "Foundations and Nonprofit Organizations." In *The Nonprofit Sector: A Research Handbook*, ed. W. W. Powell, 360–79. New Haven, CT: Yale University Press.

Zabin, Laurie, and Sarah Hayward. 1993. *Adolescent Sexual Behavior and Childbearing*. Newbury Park, CA: Sage Publications.

Zammuto, Raymond, Blair Gifford, and Eric Goodman. 2000. "Managerial Ideologies, Organization Culture, and the Outcomes of Innovation." In *Handbook of Organizational Culture and Climate*, ed. N. Ashkanasy, C. Wilderom, and M. Peterson, 263–80. London: Sage Publications.

Zoll, Daniel. 1998. "The Economic Cleansing of San Francisco." *San Francisco Bay Guardian*, October 7, 3.

Index

abortion, 42, 160n6
Adams, Natalie G., 139
African Americans. *See* Blacks
African dance, 131, 133–135, 137
Africentric womanist femininity, 67–75,
  99–117
  Afrocentricity compared to, 70–71
  Black herstory, importance of,
    102–103
  dis-identification with hypersexualized
    representations of Black femininity,
    117, 148
  empowerment discourse in, 75
  feelings of sisterhood within GEP,
    86–88
  GEP girls' challenges to, 4, 139
  GEP girls' empowerment, 94
  key qualities, 100
  middle-class perspectives and priori-
    ties, emphasis on, 75
  as politics of respectability, 113–117
  principles of, 67–68
  role model for, Lauryn Hill as,
    113–114
  self-definition in, 100–105, 125, 147
  self-determination in, 100, 105–108,
    125, 147
  self-love in, 103–105
  sexual agency in, 100, 108–113, 139,
    147
  sexual displays as challenges to, 139
  stratification of Black femininities in,
    113

Sun Valley tenants' response to, 74
Walker's influence on, Alice, 71
West African dance in, 131, 133–135,
  137
Afrocentricity, 57–59
  Africentric womanist femininity com-
    pared to, 70–71
  Black males, championing of, 58
  culture of poverty discourse, 74
  development of, 161n2
  ethnic pride, 59
  GEP women's understanding of,
    68–69
Aid to Families with Dependent Chil-
  dren (AFDC)
  Black girls' and women's sexuality, 40
  Blacks as a percentage of AFDC
    clients in Bay City, 20
  in mid-1970s, 159n2.ch2
American Association of University
  Women (AAUW), 44, 59–60,
  162n4
Americorps, 80, 163n3
Anderson, Elijah, 55–56, 121–122, 137
Angelou, Maya, 73

Badu, Erykah, 114
Baker, Josephine, 2
Bartmann, Sarah, 2, 164n1
Bay City [pseudonym], Blacks in, 20–21
  See also Sun Valley housing project
Best, Amy, 92
BET cable network, videos on, 158n11

181